Anatomicum

For my parents
KW

For Hannah
JZP

Text copyright © 2019 by Jennifer Z. Paxton
Illustrations copyright © 2019 by Katy Wiedemann

First US edition 2020
First published by Big Picture Press, an imprint of Bonnier Books UK 2019

Library of Congress Catalog Card Number pending
ISBN 978-1-5362-1506-9

20 21 22 23 24 25 WKT 10 9 8 7 6 5 4 3 2 1

Printed in Shenzhen, Guangdong, China

This book was typeset in Gill Sans and Mrs Green.
The illustrations were done in ink and watercolor.

BIG PICTURE PRESS
an imprint of
Candlewick Press
99 Dover Street
Somerville, Massachusetts 02144

www.candlewick.com

Welcome to the Museum

ADMIT ALL

Anatomicum

illustrated by KATY WIEDEMANN

written by JENNIFER Z. PAXTON

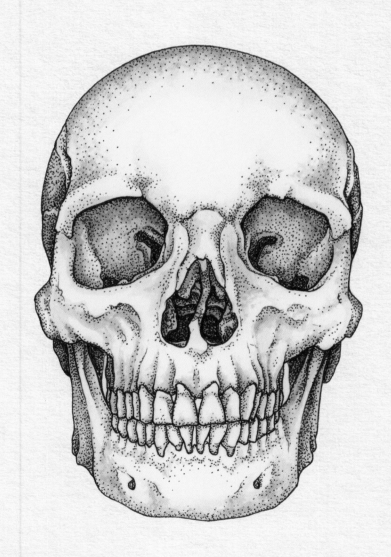

BPP

Preface

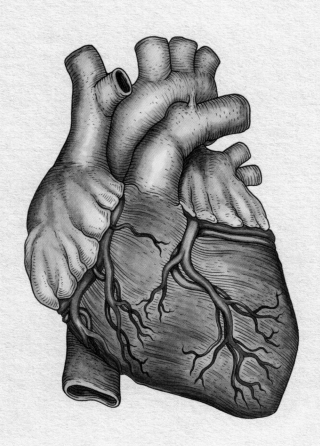

Underneath our skin lies the incredible world of the human body: a living machine constructed from hundreds and thousands of parts, all working together to make us who we are.

Exactly how our bodies work has fascinated scientists for centuries. Their study of the body's structure — called anatomy — provides the basis for all of our medical understanding.

The word *anatomy* comes from the ancient Greek *anatome*, meaning "to cut up." It has been studied since the earliest recorded periods of history, as long ago as 1600 BCE. In certain societies, the art of dissection — the "cutting up" that gives anatomy its name — was forbidden, and animal remains were dissected instead. This led to some mistakes in the understanding of the human body until years later, when scientists such as Leonardo da Vinci and Andreas Vesalius made detailed drawings of their findings. Dissection is still used by scientists and doctors as the primary way of studying the body.

Beside moral and religious concerns about dissection, there were other obstacles to early studies of anatomy and medicine. Before the development of the microscope in the 1590s, bacteria and other tiny cells were unknown to scientists. Instead, doctors believed that bad airs called "miasmas" were to blame for illnesses, and sadly, diseases that can easily be cured today killed thousands of people.

Today, we are entering an exciting new era in anatomy. Technological improvements in imaging enable us to see the human body in greater detail than ever before, and the science of tissue engineering (the building of new tissues and organs in laboratories) could help doctors find new treatments to help their patients. Every year, research leaps forward, cures are discovered, and our knowledge improves. But it all starts here, with the basics of anatomy and the study of the incredible human body.

Dr. Jennifer Z. Paxton
The University of Edinburgh

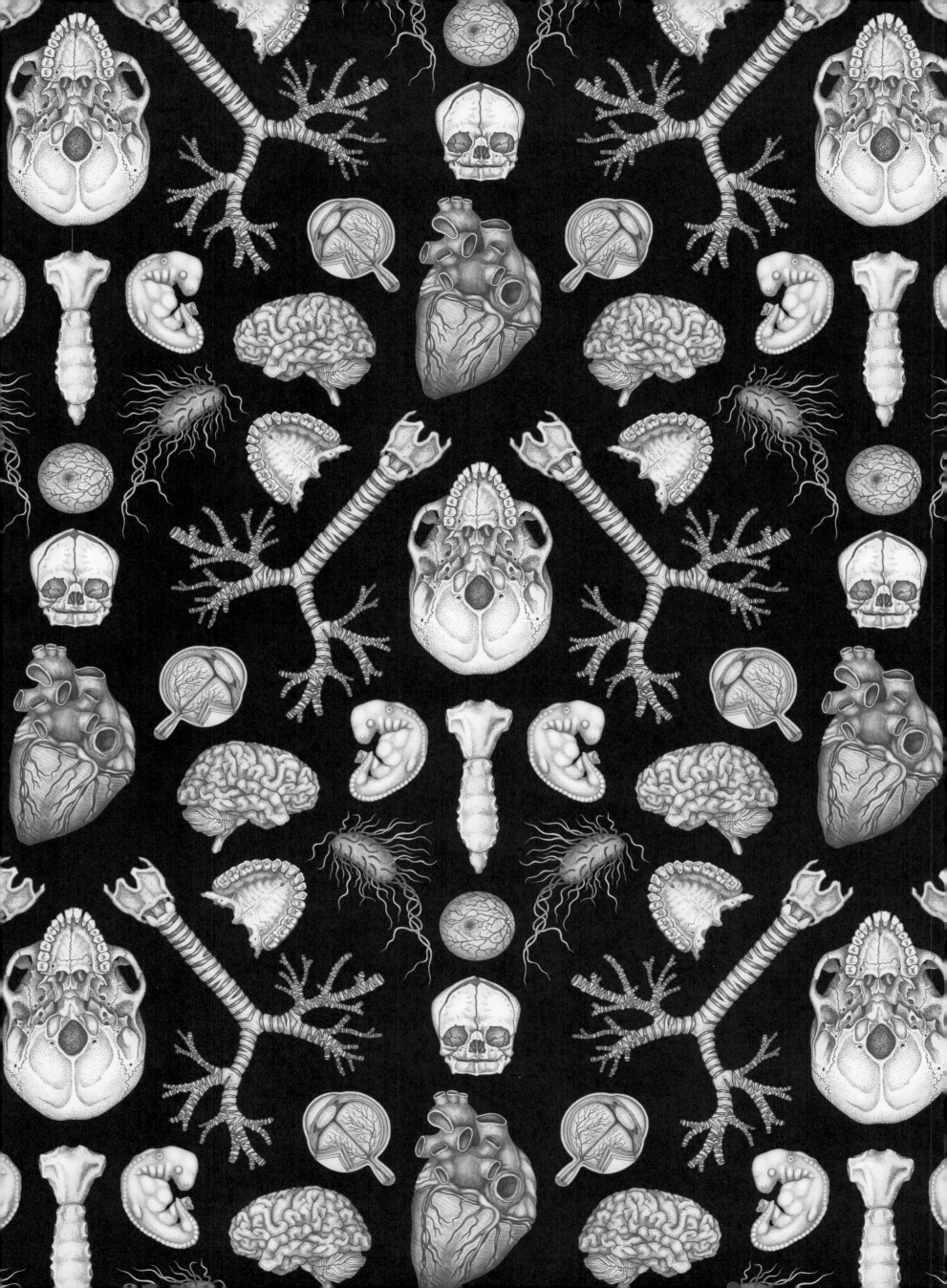

Entrance

Welcome to Anatomicum

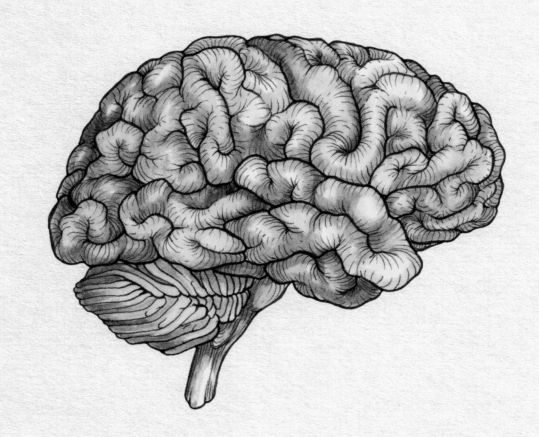

Have you ever wondered what the inside of your body looks like? Imagine you could watch your heart beating, witness your skin cells growing, or pinpoint the part of your brain where a thought takes shape. Now you can, within the pages of *Anatomicum*.

Open twenty-four hours a day, seven days a week, this unique museum isn't like anywhere you've ever been. As you walk its halls and corridors, you will be transported around the human body, seeing it in vivid detail like never before.

In each gallery you will encounter one of the body's major systems. For example, you can visit the Musculoskeletal System Gallery to discover the tissues that help us to move, or arrive at the Nervous System Gallery to examine the structure of the human brain. The exhibits will allow you to peer beneath the skin and view the organs that help us breathe, or see how food is transported and processed through the long passages of our guts. You will also learn how babies develop from a single cell and how our bodies change as we grow up.

As you explore the museum, consider how your own body is constantly working. Your heart keeps your blood pumping. Your lungs bring air in and out of your body. Every movement—and even standing still—requires actions of your muscles. Your brain processes all of the new information at astonishing speeds. Your body is amazing.

So enter *Anatomicum* here to begin your voyage of discovery and uncover the wonders and secrets of the human body.

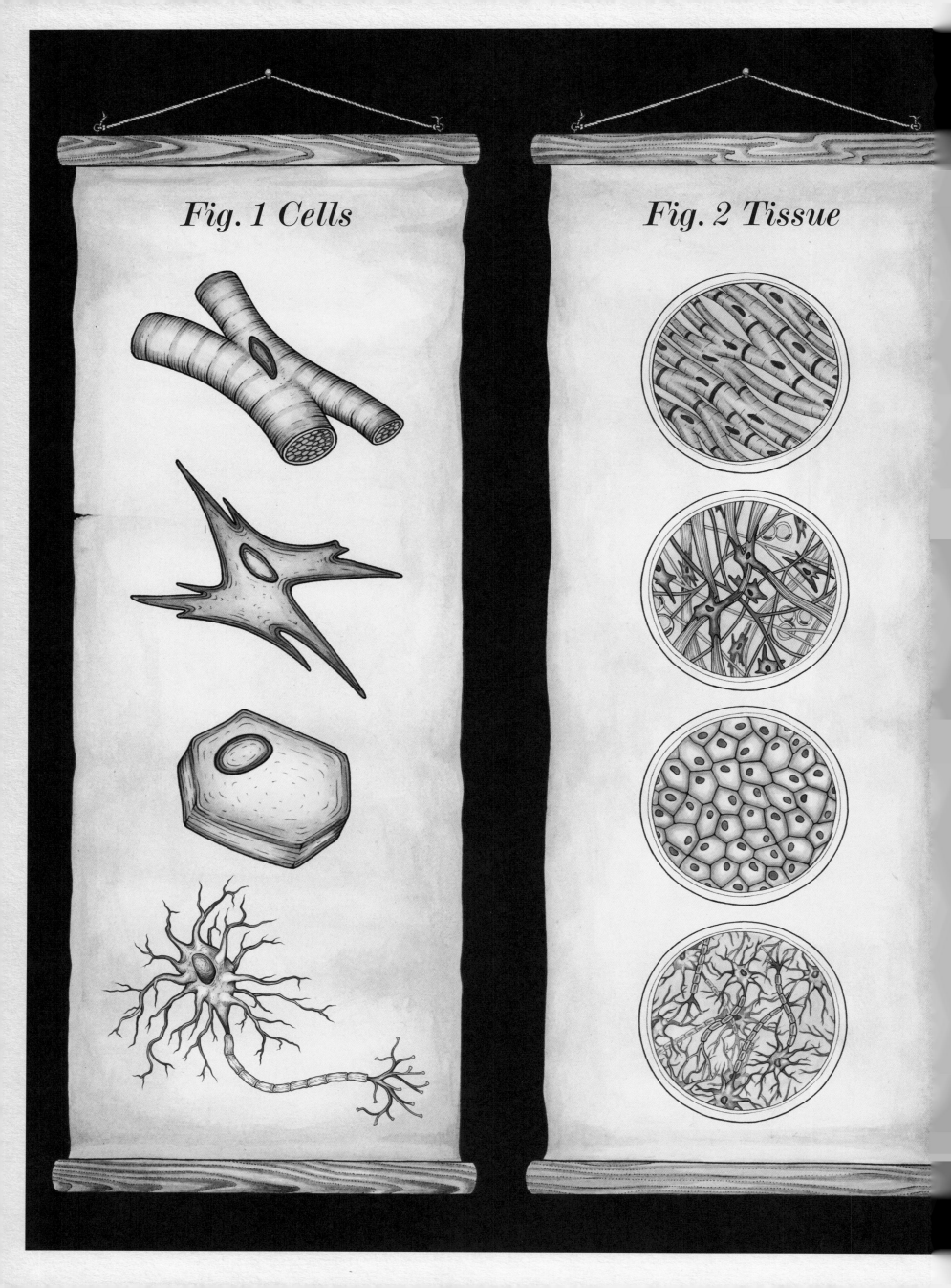

Fig. 1 Cells

Fig. 2 Tissue

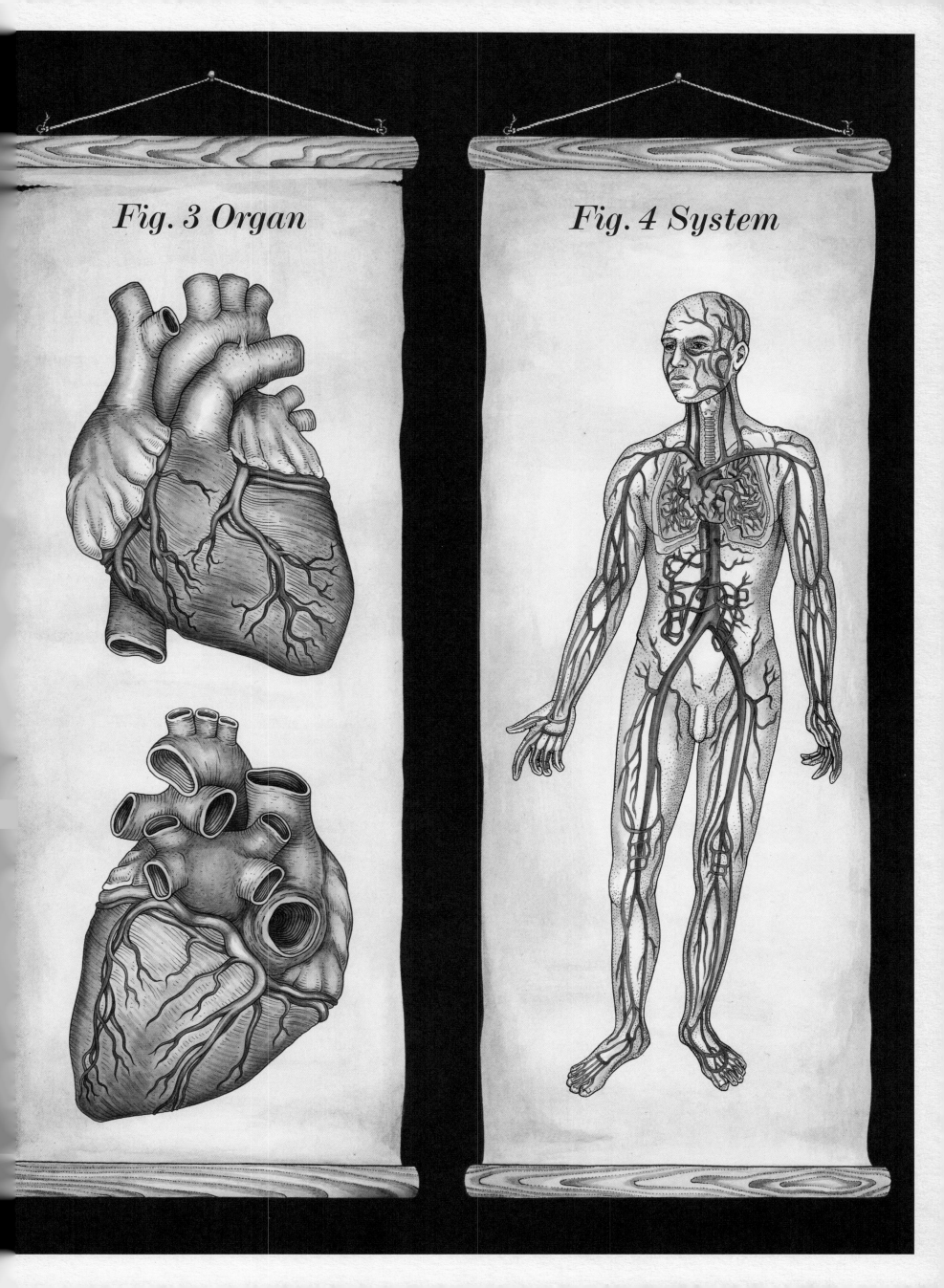

Fig. 3 Organ

Fig. 4 System

Building Blocks of the Body

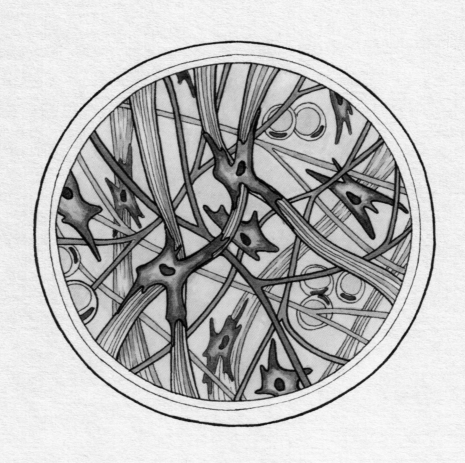

The human body is intricately detailed—woven together from individual organs, tissues, blood vessels, nerves, and cells. In anatomy, the different parts of the body are arranged from the smallest to the largest, in a simple structured order.

The smallest individual building blocks of the body are cells. An astonishing 38 trillion of them exist in the human body, each with its own special job to do. Almost every one contains DNA (deoxyribonucleic acid), the coded genetic information that determines our characteristics and makes us all unique. Individual cells can only be viewed using microscopes.

Groups of cells join together to make body tissues, which are large enough to be seen without a microscope. Epithelial tissues line the inside of organs and tubes and cover the outer surface of the skin. Muscle tissue is like the machinery of the body, making up the structures that help us to move. Nervous tissue is important for communication throughout the body, linking its different parts to the central control center of the brain. Lastly, connective tissues help to link or support different parts of the body and hold it together.

At the next level up, multiple tissue types combine to make organs: individual parts of the body with defined names and functions, such as the heart, lungs, brain, and kidneys.

Finally, several organs link up to make body systems. There are eleven systems in the human body: skeletal, muscular, digestive, cardiovascular, respiratory, urinary, nervous, integumentary, immune, reproductive, and endocrine. Each system looks after a series of related jobs, such as breathing in the respiratory system or processing food in the digestive system. Although they have individual roles, the systems all function together in harmony to keep our bodies working properly.

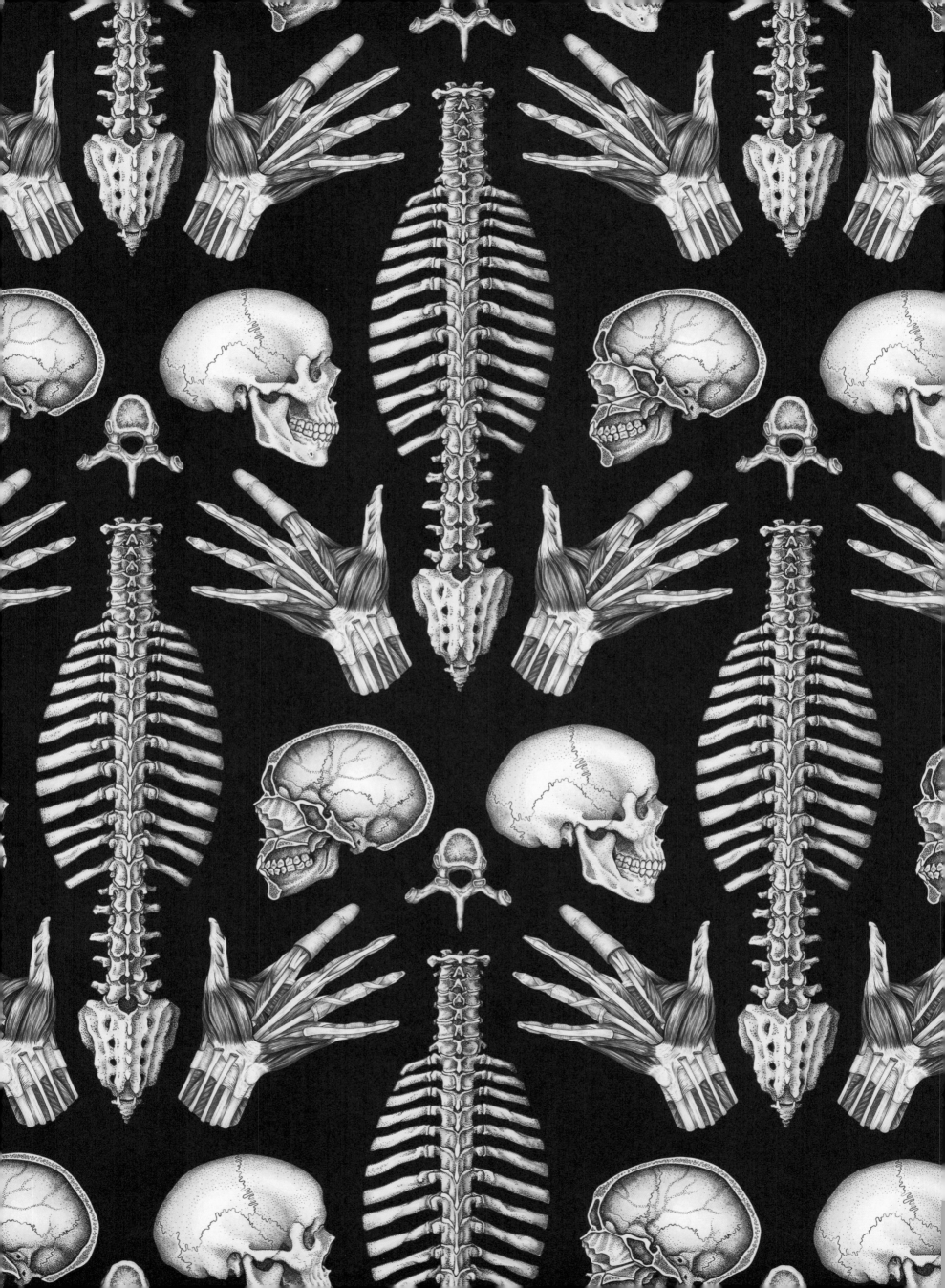

Gallery 1

The Musculoskeletal System

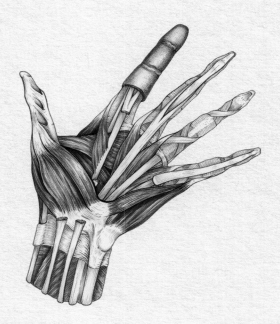

The Skeletal System

The skeleton is the framework for the entire human body. This hard but flexible scaffold gives us our overall shape, supports the muscles, protects the body's soft inner organs, and constantly manufactures new blood cells. The entire skeleton is made up of 206 individual bones, which link together at areas called joints. These keep the bones of the skeleton fixed to one another while also allowing us to move.

Anatomists categorize the skeleton in two ways. The appendicular skeleton is made up of the bones in the limbs, shoulders, and pelvis. The axial skeleton consists of all the bones of the head and trunk. The primary role of the axial skeleton is to protect the brain, the sensory organs (eyes, ears, mouth, and nose), the heart, and the lungs. The axial skeleton also includes the spine, a long row of thirty-three bones called vertebrae that encase the delicate spinal cord. Stacked together, the vertebrae make a curved, flexible pillar, which can bend forward, backward, or from side to side. This vertebral column connects to the skull at its first (or top) vertebra, which is named after the figure Atlas from ancient Greek mythology. Atlas bore the weight of the whole sky on his shoulders, just as the atlas vertebra has to support the weight of the skull and brain.

The bones of the upper limbs—the arm, forearm, wrist, and hand—have a greater range of movement than any other part of the skeleton, combining strength with dexterity so that we can perform tasks as varied as threading a needle and batting a ball. In contrast, the bones of the lower limbs—the thigh, leg, ankle, and foot—mainly provide stability and support our weight as we walk, stand, or run. Key to this is the longest and strongest bone in the human body: the femur or thigh bone.

Key to plate

1: **Skeleton, seen from the front (anterior view)**

a) Cranium (skull bones)
b) Clavicle (collar bone)
c) Sternum (breast bone)
d) Humerus (arm bone)
e) Ribs
f) Pelvis (hip bones)
g) Ulna (inner forearm bone)
h) Radius (outer forearm bone)
i) Femur (thigh bone)
j) Patella (kneecap)
k) Tibia (inner leg bone)
l) Fibula (outer leg bone)
m) Tarsal bones (ankle and foot bones)
n) Metatarsals (bones of the foot)
o) Phalanges (toe bones)

2: **Skeleton, seen from the back (posterior view)**

a) Atlas (first spine bone)
b) Axis (second spine bone)
c) Vertebral column (spine or backbone)
d) Scapula (shoulder blade)
e) Carpal bones (wrist bones)
f) Metacarpals (hand bones)
g) Phalanges (finger bones)
h) Ilium (one of the pelvis bones)
i) Sacrum (fused bones at base of spine)
j) Coccyx (tail bone)
k) Calcaneus (heel bone)

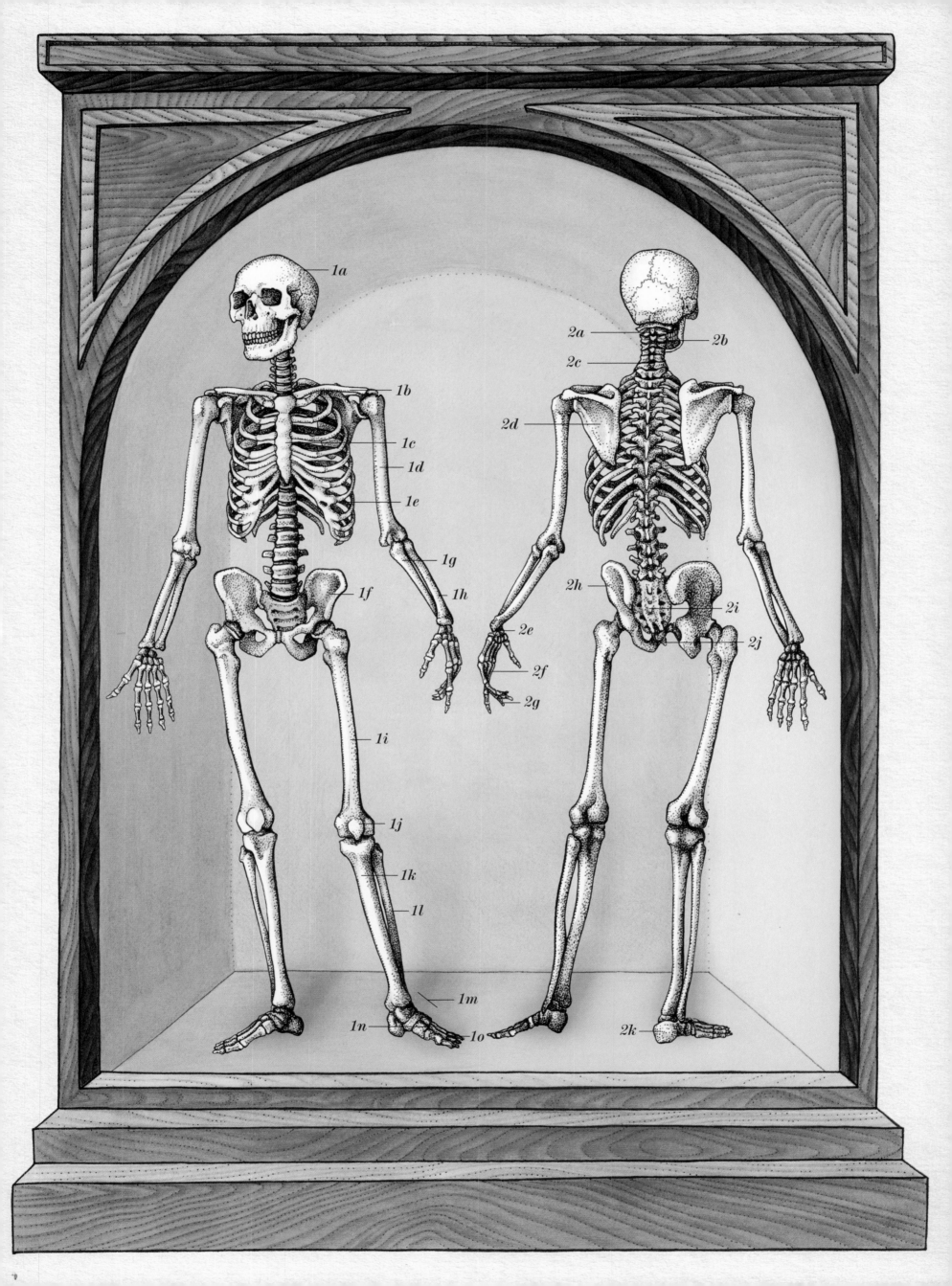

Bones

Bones come in all shapes and sizes, but can be roughly grouped into five types: long, short, flat, sesamoid, and irregular. Long bones, such as those in the thigh, usually support the body's weight. Short bones, found in the wrist and ankle, are roughly cube-shaped and support the joints. Flat bones, like the bones of the skull, are thin and curved and protect the body's organs. Sesamoid bones (named after their resemblance to sesame seeds), such as the patella in the knee, are small, round bones sometimes found at joints. All other types are described as irregular bones, which have complex shapes designed for specific jobs, like the bones of the vertebral column.

All bones are made from a substance called mineralized collagen that is a mixture of calcium minerals, which make bones sturdy, and collagen, which makes bones a little springy. This combination ensures bones are strong while preventing them from snapping under pressure. It is thought that, when comparing weight for weight, bone is around four times stronger than concrete and more resilient than a steel bar.

For hundreds of years, scientists thought bones were dry and lifeless, but today we know they are constantly growing and responding to the environment around them. We are born with over 300 bones, but as we age, some of these fuse together to make the 206 bones of the adult skeleton. Bones have the ability to repair themselves, too. A rich blood supply ensures nutrients are directed straight to the damaged area of any bone, and most fractures take just six weeks to heal. Bones also respond to our lifestyle. More bone is produced after exercise. For example, tennis players often have stronger bones in their serving arm compared to their other arm. In contrast, inactivity during long periods of illness or an astronaut's time in space makes bones weaker and more likely to fracture. This shows that the best way to keep strong, healthy bones is to exercise regularly.

───────────────── *Key to plate* ─────────────────

1: **Vertebra**
a) Single vertebra (viewed from above): Vertebrae are irregularly shaped bones. They protect the spinal cord, which runs through a hole in the middle of the vertebra called the vertebral foramen, and provide support for the upper body.
b) Vertebral column and ribs (from behind): The vertebral column, or spine, is made up of thirty-three individual vertebrae. Twelve of them articulate, or connect, with our twenty-four ribs.

2: **Bones of the right knee region, seen from the front (anterior view)**
a) Femur
b) Tibia

c) Patella: a sesamoid bone
d) Fibula

3: **Bones of the right foot, seen from below (inferior view)**
The twenty-six bones of the foot have a variety of shapes and sizes. The tarsal bones that make up the ankle region are short bones that fit together.

4: **Sternum, seen from the front (anterior view)**
The sternum, or breastbone, is a flat bone at the front of the rib cage. Looking a little like a tie, it joins the cartilage of the ribs on both sides of the chest together and helps to protect the delicate heart and lungs underneath it.

5: **Femur**
a) Seen from the back (posterior view): The rounded ball at the top of this long bone is the femoral head, which forms part of the hip joint.
b) Cross section of femur seen from the front: The long bone of the femur contains a long shaft between the two rounded ends. The outer surface of the shaft is made from compact bone *(i)*, which is hard and strong. Air-filled spongy or cancellous bone *(ii)* found at the rounded ends is lighter and more flexible. A medullary cavity *(iii)* runs through the shaft, containing blood vessels, nerves, and bone marrow, where blood cells are made.

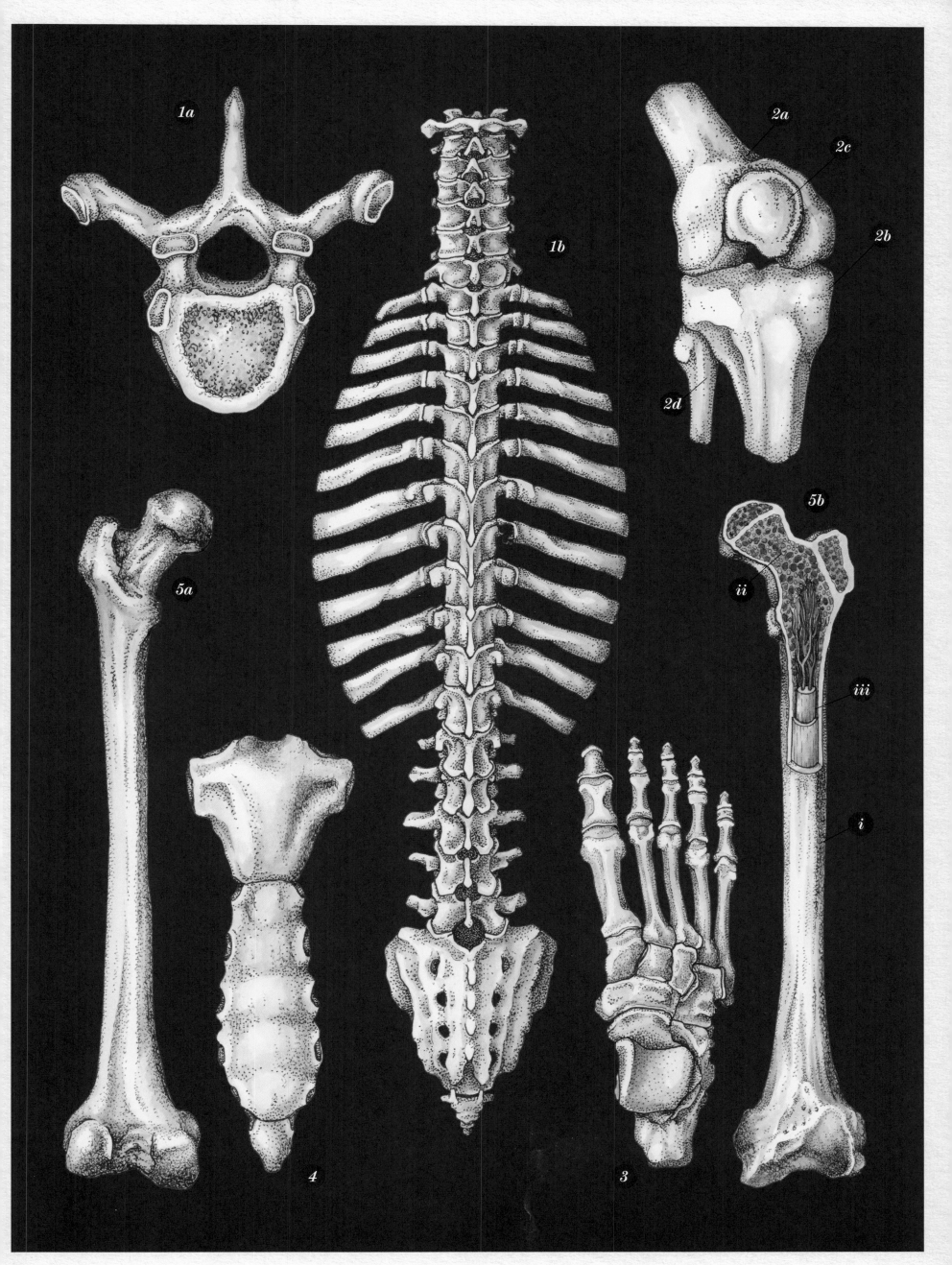

The Skull

Underneath the skin and muscles of our head lies the skull, a protective home for the brain and sensory organs (the eyes, ears, nose, and tongue). Although the skull appears to be a single bone, it is formed by twenty-two individual bones, most of which are fused together at immovable joints known as sutures. The top part, or vault, is formed by eight bones and functions like a helmet, protecting the brain inside from injury. The other fourteen bones provide shape for the face and jaw. Only one of these, the mandible or jawbone, can move. This bone is joined to the skull by a hinge joint, letting us open and close the jaw when chewing and talking.

Most of the bones in the face have air-filled spaces within them called sinuses. These reduce the overall weight of the skull and add a deeper, clearer sound to our voices during speech by allowing air to vibrate within them. In addition to sinuses, there are a number of holes running right through the skull bones, known as foramina. These let the brain connect with other parts of the body via nerves and allow blood vessels to pass between the head and the rest of the body. At the base of the skull, the foramen magnum, meaning "great hole," is where the brain joins to the spinal cord.

You might notice there are no ears or nose visible. This is because the shape of the outer nose and ear is made from cartilage, a material that is softer than bone.

Scientists known as paleoanthropologists can study bones to discover facts about ancient cultures, while forensic osteologists study bones to uncover vital clues about the cause of death in criminal cases. We can ascertain age, gender, and ethnicity by studying the skull's size and features, and, as with other bones, it is possible to see what diseases a person may have suffered from or even where they may have lived.

----------------------------------- *Key to plate* -----------------------------------

1: **Adult skull**

a) From the front

b) From the back: The sagittal *(i)* and lambdoid *(ii)* sutures join the parietal *(iii)* and occipital *(iv)* skull bones together.

c) From the base (without jaw): The large central hole in the base of the skull is called the foramen magnum. This is the point where the spinal cord passes out of the skull to travel down the vertebral column.

d) From the side: The coronal *(i)*, squamous *(ii)*, and lambdoid *(iii)* sutures join the frontal *(iv)*, parietal

(v), temporal *(vi)*, and occipital *(vii)* skull bones together.

e) Cross section from the side: The space inside the skull where the brain sits is called the cranial fossa.

2: **Newborn skull**

In babies, joints of the skull have not yet hardened. The sutures are made from a much more flexible material, creating "soft spots" or fontanelles in a baby's skull. Babies' brains grow rapidly as they develop, from only about 12 ounces/350 grams at birth to nearly 21 ounces/600 grams in the first three

months—about half the size of an adult brain. Fontanelles mean that the skull can easily cope with this rapid growth.

a) From the top: The diamond-shaped area is the main fontanelle *(i)* of a baby's skull.

b) From the front: Infant skulls display a more prominent forehead and orbits and a smaller jaw than the typical adult skull.

c) From the side: The prominent forehead and the shape of the small jaw are noticeable.

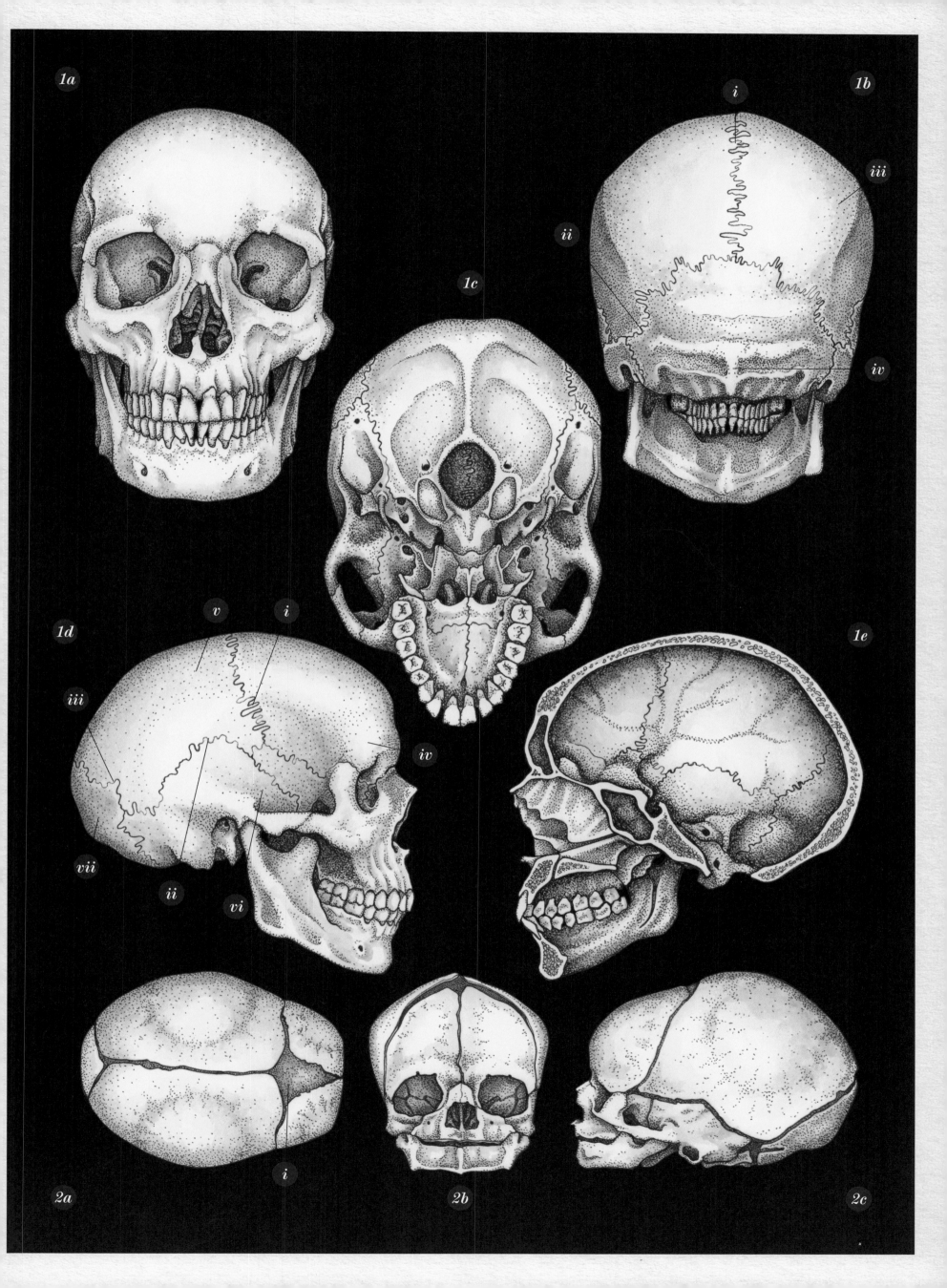

Joints

Joints, or articulations, are the points where two or more bones link together in the skeleton. There are over 300 joints in the body, and every bone is connected to at least one other, with the exception of the hyoid bone in the throat. Although joints are often thought of as the movable parts of the skeleton, there are actually three different types, ranging from movable to completely rigid.

Fibrous or immovable joints serve the important function of holding bones together for stability. For example, the bones of the adult skull come together at the sutures, which are fibrous joints. Fibrous joints also hold teeth securely in place in their bony sockets.

Slightly more flexible than these is a group known as cartilaginous joints, where a layer of cartilage, a tissue softer than bone, sits between the bones and joins them together. These exist between the ribs and the breastbone, between the two sides of the pelvis, and between the vertebrae of the spine. As these joints allow for a little movement, the bones can shift position slightly when needed. For instance, the joints in the pelvis become more flexible during pregnancy, enabling women to give birth more easily.

By far the most common type of joints are the movable, or synovial, joints, including the hip, knee, shoulder, and elbow. Although each joint has a unique shape, the basic structure is the same in all synovial joints. The ends of the bones are covered in a layer of hyaline cartilage, which helps to reduce friction as the bones slide past each other. The bones are held together by tough bands of tissue called ligaments, while a strong but flexible capsule wraps around the joint like a cuff to help keep it together. These joints also contain a slippery liquid called synovial fluid, which keeps them well lubricated, a bit like using oil to help a metal hinge move more easily. The sound of your knees popping or your knuckles cracking is the sound of air bubbles in the synovial fluid bursting. It is completely harmless.

Key to plate

1: Pivot joint
In pivot joints, one bone rotates around another. A good example is the joint between the atlas and the axis in the vertebral column. It is used to turn the head from side to side.

2: Ball-and-socket joint
This joint gets its name from the "ball" of one bone, usually a long bone, fitting into a corresponding "socket" on the adjoining bone. It allows movements in lots of different directions (bending, rotation, etc.). Some examples are the shoulder and hip joints.

3: Hinge joint
Hinge joints allow movement in one direction only and act just like hinges on doors to allow bending but not rotation. Major hinge joints of the body are at the elbows, knees, and ankle joints.

4: Condyloid joint
These are found where one bone is rounded and fits into a shallow depression on its neighboring bone. Condyloid joints, also known as ellipsoidal joints, allow movements in many directions, such as the movements of the wrist.

5: Saddle joint
Resembling a saddle on top of another bone, these joints allow side-to-side and bending movement, but no rotation. They include the joint between the carpals and metacarpals of the thumb.

6: Planar joint
Also called gliding joints, these occur where bones lie flat against each other. They allow bones to slide from side to side or up and down. Planar joints are found between the bones in the wrist and ankle regions.

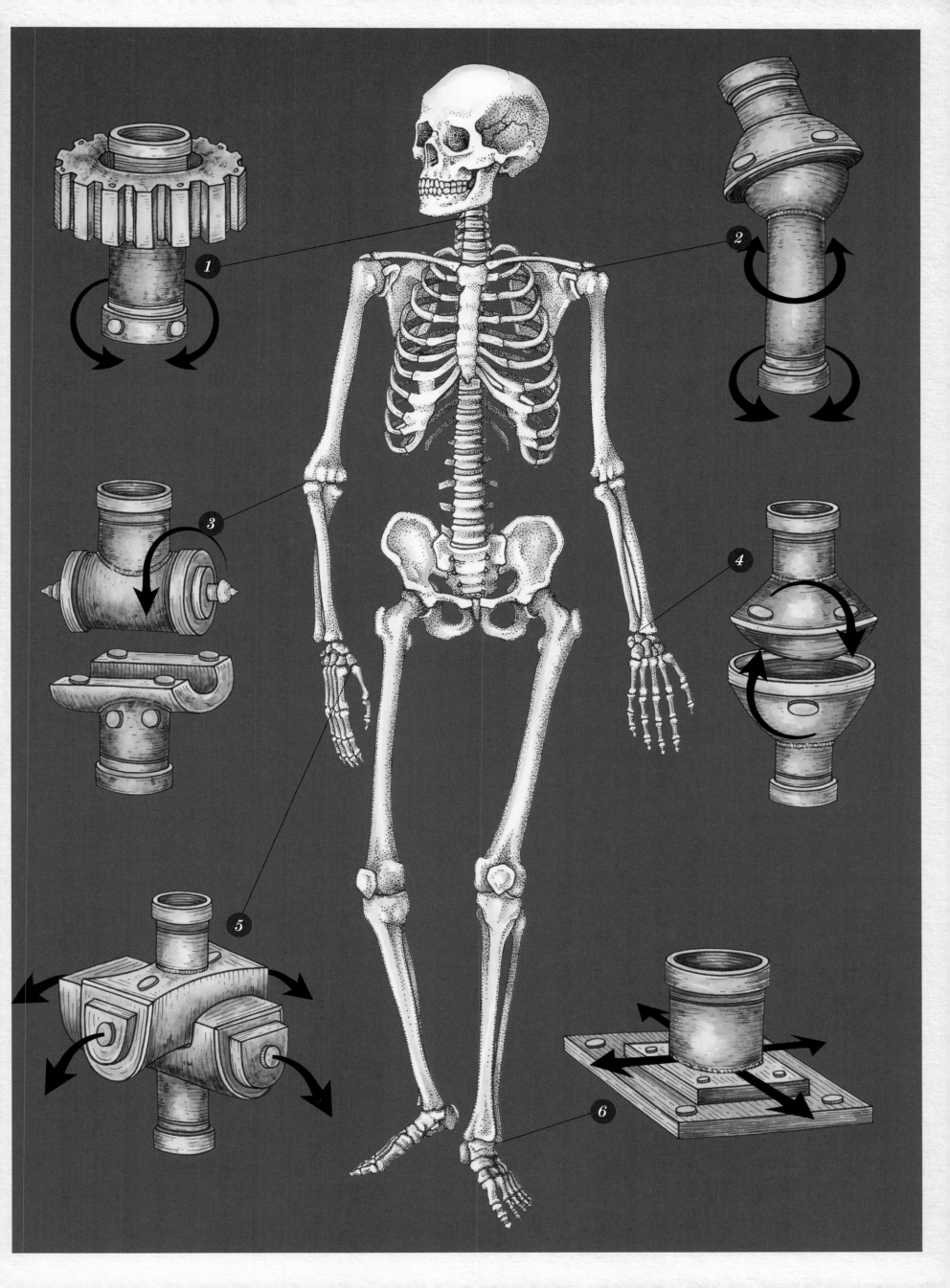

Connective Tissues

Bones and muscles are not the only tissues in the skeletal system. Joining bones to bones, and attaching bones to muscles, are a number of connective tissues—tendons, ligaments, and cartilage—that link, support, and protect the entire skeleton.

Tendons are thick straps of tissue attaching muscle to bone. When a muscle contracts, it shortens, pulling on the tendon so that it moves the bone. Tendons are made from a protein called collagen, with long fibers side by side in a structure resembling a thick, strong, stretchy rope.

Ligaments have a similar rope-like structure and are also made from collagen. However, instead of connecting muscle to bone, ligaments link bone to bone, helping to keep joints stable. For example, the bones of the knees do not slot together very well, so the knee joint has ligaments inside and outside the joint to help provide stability.

While tendons and ligaments are strong when they are pulled, cartilage, a soft, flexible substance found all over the body, is strongest when it is pressed. There are three types of cartilage. Hyaline, or articulating, cartilage is found on the surface of bones in movable joints, where it acts as a shock absorber and reduces friction between bones. Fibrocartilage is very strong tissue found in soft discs between the vertebrae of the spine and between the bones of the knee joint. Lastly, elastic cartilage is a specialized bouncy tissue found in the epiglottis, auditory tube, and outer ear.

Key to plate

1: **Knee joint and leg (without muscles), seen from the front and side (anterior and lateral view)**
a) Quadriceps tendon: This joins the quadriceps muscle to the tibia (shin bone) and holds the patella.
b) Patella (kneecap)
c) Fibular collateral ligament: This connects the femur to the fibula.
d) Cartilage: This sits on the surface of bones where they meet other bones in the skeleton. Its role is to reduce friction.
e) The anterior and posterior cruciate ligaments: These sit inside the knee joint and join the femur and tibia together.

f) The patellar ligament: This joins the patella to the tibia.
g) Ligaments of the ankle joint: These help to hold the ankle bones together for stability.

2: **Knee joint and leg (with muscles), seen from the back (posterior view)**
a) Gastrocnemius muscle (calf muscle)
b) Achilles tendon: The largest and strongest tendon in the body, which can easily be felt at the back of the heel. It joins the gastrocnemius muscle (calf muscle) to the heel bone. When the muscle contracts, it lifts the heel bone upward to pull us up onto our

tiptoes. The tendon is named after the ancient Greek warrior Achilles, who was said to be immortal after being dipped in the river Styx as a baby. The only part of him untouched by the water was his heel, as this was where his mother held him. Achilles was later killed after being shot in the heel with an arrow—his only weak spot (and the origin of the expression "Achilles' heel"). The naming of the Achilles tendon calls to mind how vulnerable we are if this crucial tendon becomes injured.
c) Calcaneus (heel bone)

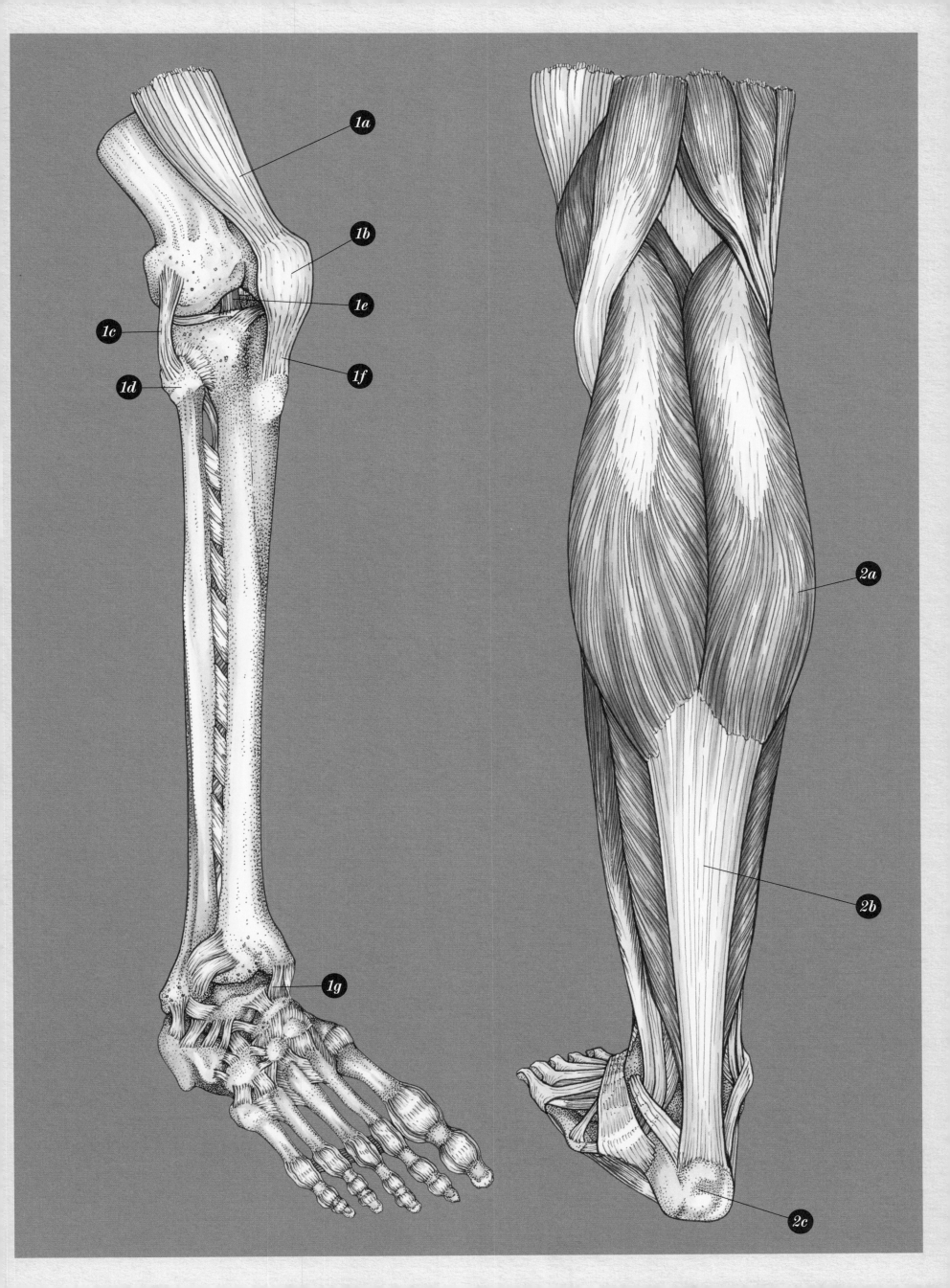

The Muscular System

From the cautious first steps of a baby finding its way in the world to the speed of an Olympic athlete or the grace of a ballet dancer, the muscular system is responsible for producing every possible kind of movement.

Found throughout the body in three types—skeletal, cardiac, and smooth—all muscle tissue shares one important feature: the ability to contract, or shorten, to make part of the body move. In skeletal muscle, contractions pull on the bones they attach to, moving them into a new position. Because these muscles can only pull in one direction, they usually work in pairs. So after one muscle contracts to bend a joint, a corresponding muscle contracts to straighten it out again. For example, when the biceps muscle in your upper arm contracts, it pulls on tendons connecting to your forearm, raising your hand and wrist upward. To lower your forearm again, the biceps relaxes and the triceps muscle on the underside of your arm contracts instead. Skeletal muscle gives the body its shape and is thought to account for around 40 percent of an adult's total body weight.

Muscle contractions produce around 70 percent of our total body heat. Cardiac muscle pumps blood and smooth muscle moves food through the digestive tract.

Key to plate

1: **Skeletal muscles, seen from the back (posterior view)**
There are over six hundred named skeletal muscles in the body. Their names follow simple rules based on the action, shape, size, or location of the muscle. *Flexor* and *extensor* are commonly used prefixes, which identify their function as flexors (for bending) or extensors (for straightening) at joints.

Scientific terms also relate to the comparative size of muscles, as in *maximus* (large), *minimus* (small),

longus (long), and *brevis* (short). The word *muscle* itself comes from the Latin for "little mouse," suggested to be because the muscle belly (the central part that bulges) and tendon (that attaches it to the bone) resemble a mouse and its tail.
a) Trapezius
b) Latissimus dorsi
c) Gluteus maximus
d) Hamstrings (semitendinosus, semimembranosus, and biceps femoris)
e) Gastrocnemius

f) Triceps brachii
g) Deltoid

2: **Skeletal muscles, seen from the front (anterior view)**
a) Pectoralis major
b) Biceps brachii
c) Rectus abdominus
d) Quadriceps (rectus femoris, vastus lateralis, vastus medialis, vastus intermedius)
e) Tibialis anterior

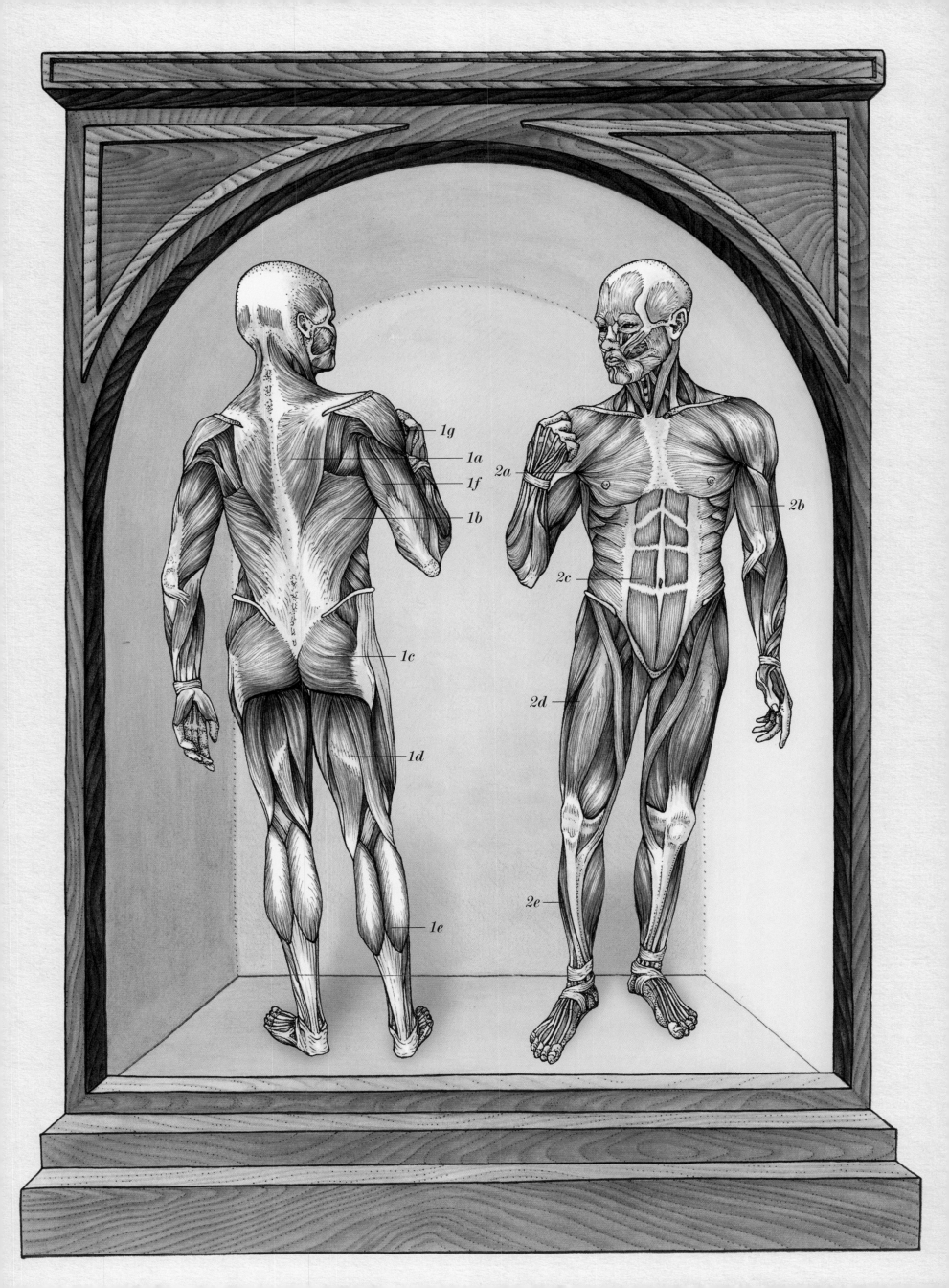

Muscle Tissue

Muscle tissue is formed by thousands of long, thin cells called myocytes, which contract together to make a muscle change shape. Skeletal, cardiac, and smooth muscle are all made of myocytes, but arranged in very different ways—some moved by involuntary control and some by voluntary control.

Skeletal muscle, which attaches to the body's skeleton, is formed of myocytes combined in long, thin strands called muscle fibers. These combine to give the shape of the "belly"—the rounded part of the muscle you can see beneath the skin. Skeletal muscles are all under voluntary control, meaning we have to think in order to move them: electrical signals are sent from the brain, via the spinal cord, to nerves within the muscle. By contrast, cardiac and smooth muscles move involuntarily without us ever having to think about them.

Cardiac muscle makes up the walls of the heart and is not found anywhere else in the body. Its role is to squeeze the heart's chambers in a steady rhythm, transporting blood all around the body. The regular squeezing occurs as electrical impulses travel through structures like wires within the muscle tissue itself.

Smooth muscle appears in the walls of blood vessels, parts of the urinary system, and the digestive tract. It is activated via signals from the nervous system and mostly controls the width of tubes or tracts, tightening or relaxing to control what's inside them. For instance, the squeezing motion known as peristalsis pushes food down the digestive tract, just like squeezing toothpaste out of a tube. Smooth muscle is also found in the walls of the bladder. In fact, the bladder has one of the only smooth muscles to be given its own name—the detrusor muscle. The detrusor muscle squeezes to push urine out. Since the bladder is made from smooth muscles, this is not under voluntary control. A valve called the external urinary sphincter lets us control where and when we empty our bladder.

Key to plate

1: Cardiac muscle

a) Heart: Cardiac muscle makes up the walls of the heart, and its contraction pumps blood around the heart and on to the lungs or the rest of the body.

b) Cardiac muscle structure: Microscopic cardiac muscle cells have a branched shape and a striated, or striped, appearance. Each cell contains an individual nucleus. Cells are joined together at areas called intercalated discs, which help transmit the electrical signal needed to contract the muscle.

2: Smooth muscle

a) Stomach: The walls of the stomach are made from three layers of smooth muscle, each oriented in a different direction. These muscles move in a churning motion to mix the stomach contents effectively.

b) Smooth muscle structure: Smooth muscle cells are long and thin cells with individual nuclei but no striations.

3: Skeletal muscle

a) Biceps brachii: All skeletal muscles have at least one origin, where the muscle originates from a bone, and an insertion point, where it attaches to another bone. Biceps brachii has two origins (in fact, *biceps* means two heads). Contraction of biceps brachii leads to bending the upper limb at the elbow.

b) Skeletal muscle structure: Skeletal muscle cells in the form of muscle fibers, each with multiple nuclei. The muscle fibers are highly striated.

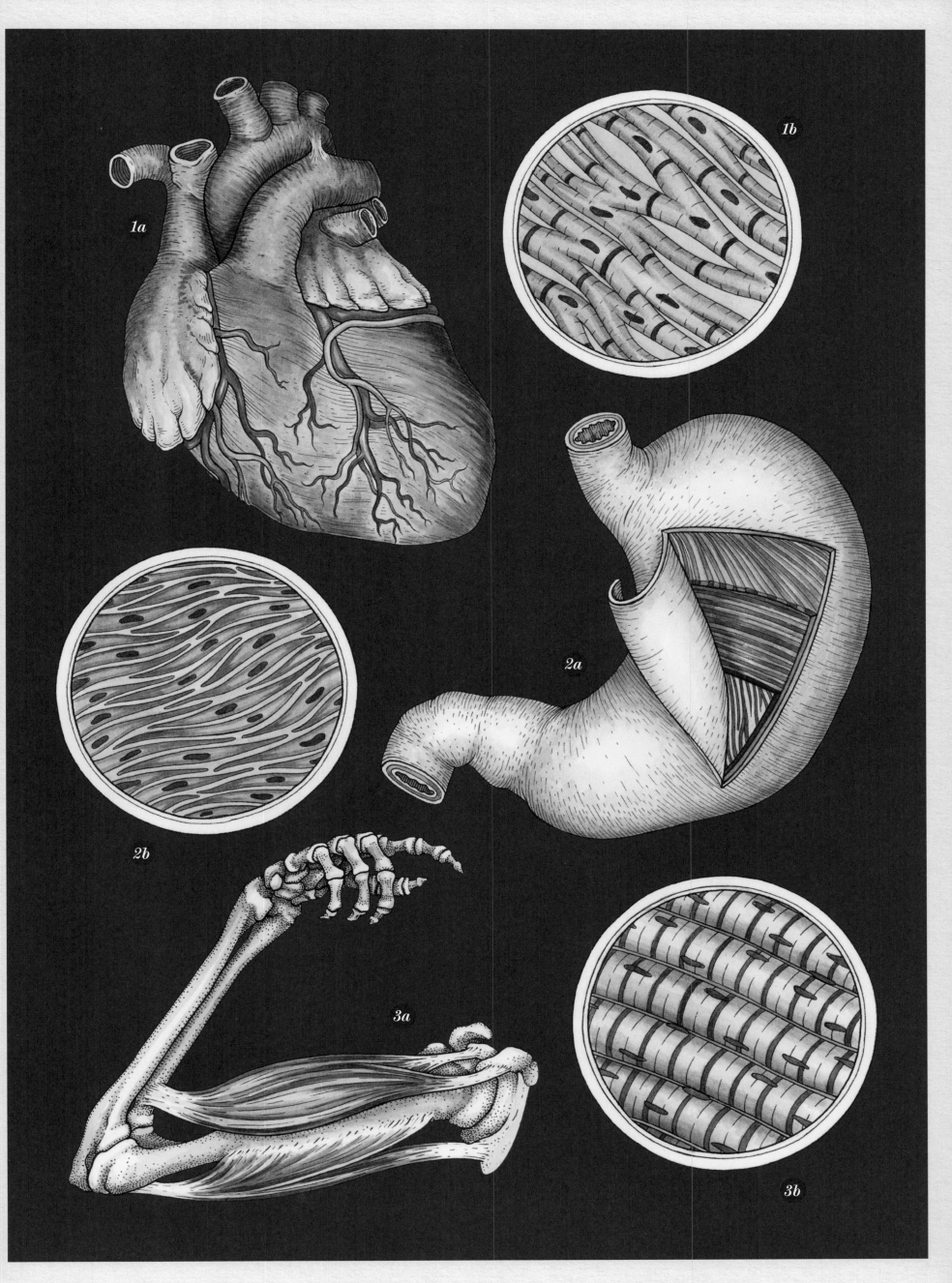

Muscles: The Hands

Most animals walk on all fours, a type of movement known as a quadrupedal gait. Humans, however, have an upright walking position, or bipedal gait. Walking on two feet has enabled our hands to evolve into functional tools. In fact, our hands, and the incredible range of movements they can perform, are key to the skills that distinguish us from other species.

Our hands are used for eating, washing, and carrying objects, as well as for communicating through hand gestures. The intricate machinery of the hand also lets us perform more specialized, complicated movements such as playing a musical instrument, holding a pencil, buttoning a shirt, or turning a key in a lock.

Interestingly, fingers themselves do not contain any muscles. Movements of the fingers are driven by muscles in the forearm and hand. The tendons of these muscles travel along the length of the fingers to the tips like long strings, carefully weaving past each other and enabling the joints to move between the finger bones. Other small muscles within the palm of the hand produce finer movements of the fingers, needed for precise actions.

One of the key movements for the usefulness of our hands is the ability to oppose the thumb. This means we can move it so that the tip of the thumb touches the tip of the little finger. In fact, the majority of hand actions we rely on every day would not be possible without our opposable thumbs.

Key to plate

1: **Bones of the left hand and wrist**
The twenty-seven bones in the hand—fourteen phalanges, five metacarpal bones, and eight carpal bones—fit together like pieces of a jigsaw puzzle.
a) Phalanges
b) Metacarpal bones
c) Carpal bones

2: **Soft tissues of the hand**
For hand and finger movements to occur, many muscles in the forearm are engaged using long tendons that extend into the fingers. These tendons are held in place under casings called sheaths that help the tendons glide smoothly during movements. There are also many muscles in the palm of the hand that help with fine motor movements.

3: **Power grip**
This type of grip is useful for carrying objects such as shopping bags or suitcases, or holding objects like a hammer or a baseball bat.

4: **Precision grips**
These grips are useful for picking up small objects and require a high level of fine motor control.
a) Pincer grip: This delicate precision grip joins the index finger and opposable thumb. It is an important grip for picking up objects.
b) Dynamic tripod grip: Often used for holding a pen, this precision grip uses the thumb, index, and middle fingers for support and control.

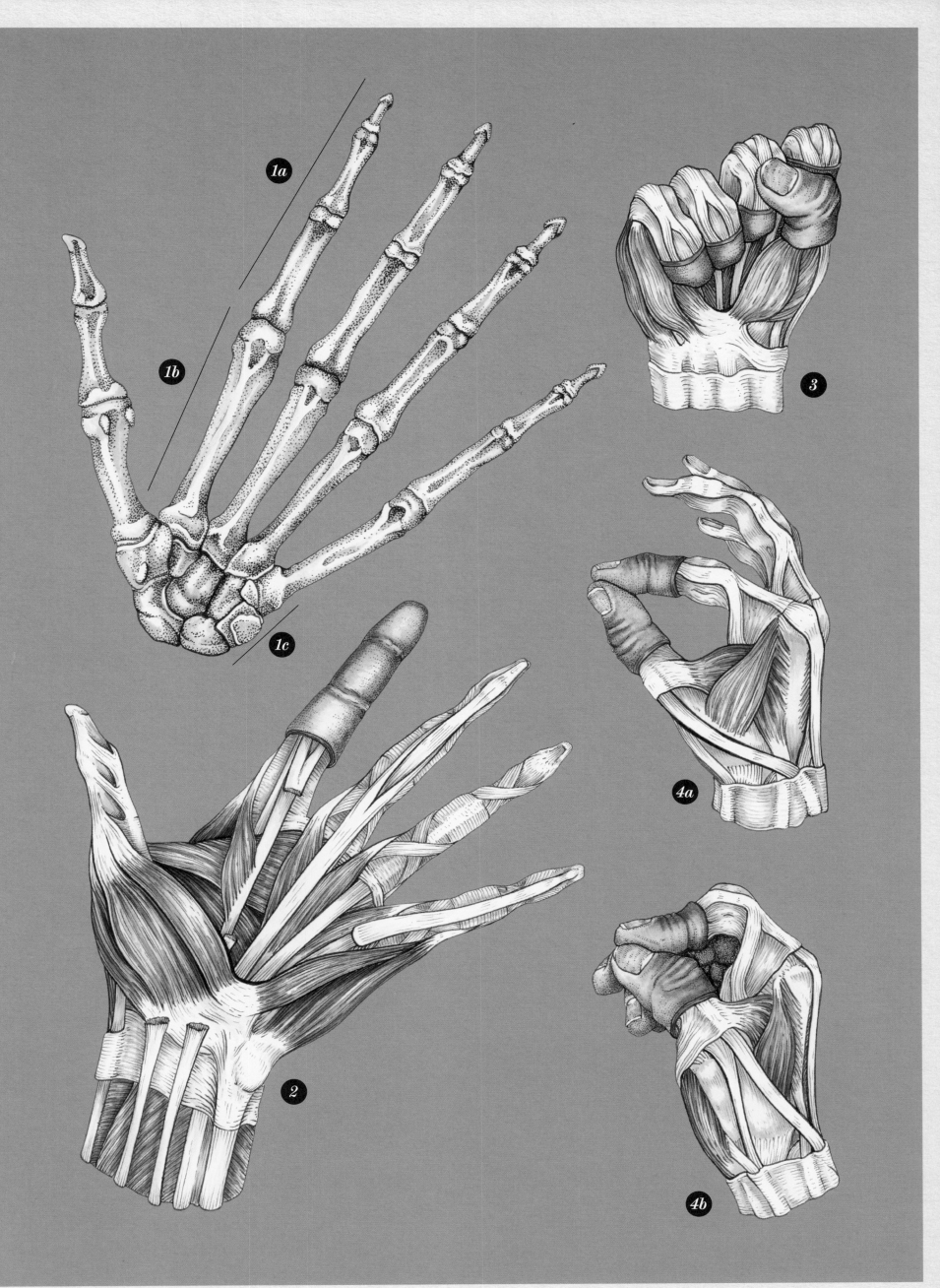

Muscles:
Facial Expression

You can often tell what emotion a person is feeling by the expression on their face. Even though we communicate with one another by speaking, we also have an excellent ability to notice and understand body language, especially facial expressions.

Our faces have over forty muscles, which join to the bones of the skull. They work together in many combinations, allowing us to produce approximately ten thousand different facial expressions, which are vital for our ability to communicate. Many of these muscles have a clear functional role, such as the muscles surrounding the eyes and mouth. The orbicularis oculi muscle circles each eye and is used to close the eyelid, with extra contraction enabling the eyes to squint. Orbicularis oris, the muscle around the mouth, is used to close and stick out the lips and is therefore known as the "kissing muscle." Both the orbicularis muscles are flat, rounded structures and are very similar in shape; in fact, their name comes from the Latin *orbis,* meaning "circular" or "disc-shaped." Other muscles can pull a part of the face up or down, such as the depressor anguli oris, which pulls the corners of the mouth downward in a frown, and the levator palpebrae superioris, used to open the eyelid. The muscle used to convey surprise is the frontalis muscle on the forehead, which pulls the eyebrows upward and wrinkles the forehead. We use many more muscles when we frown than when we smile. Real smiles of happiness also involve involuntary actions of the muscles around the eyes, not just the muscles surrounding the mouth. This means we can often tell the difference between a fake smile and a genuine one!

Key to plate

1: **Muscles of facial expression**
a) Frontalis
b) Temporalis
c) Orbicularis oculi
d) Nasalis
e) Orbicularis oris
f) Levator labii superioris
g) Zygomaticus major and minor
h) Depressor anguli oris
i) Platysma
j) Mentalis

2: **Kissing muscles**
The orbicularis oris muscle closes and protrudes the lips as when kissing.

3: **Muscles of smiling and winking**
The zygomaticus major pulls the corners of the mouth upward when smiling. In winking, the orbicularis oculi muscle contracts to close the eyelid. The orbicularis oculi muscles also contract involuntarily when you smile.

4: **Muscles of sadness**
The depressor anguli oris pulls the corners of the mouth downward.

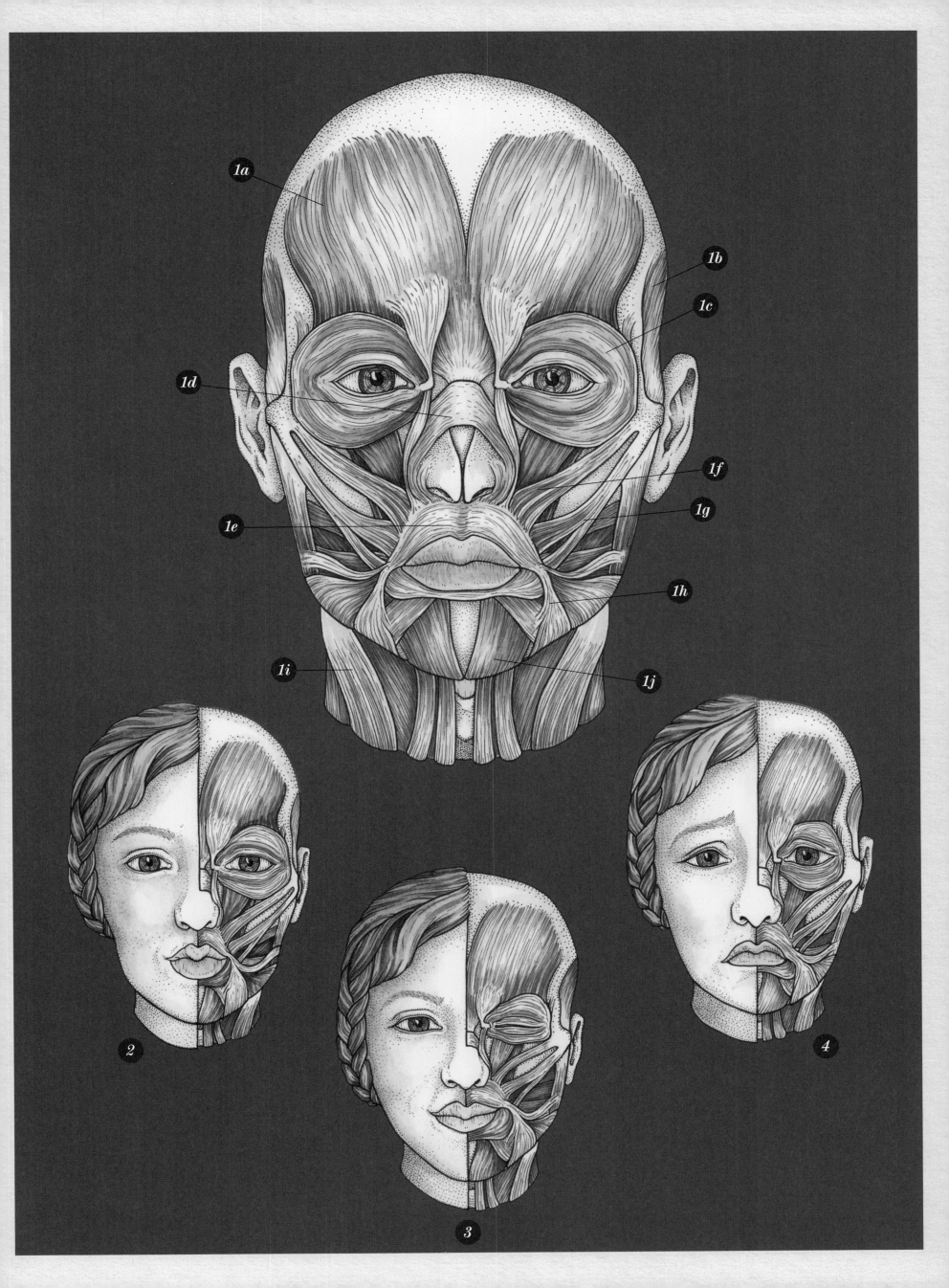

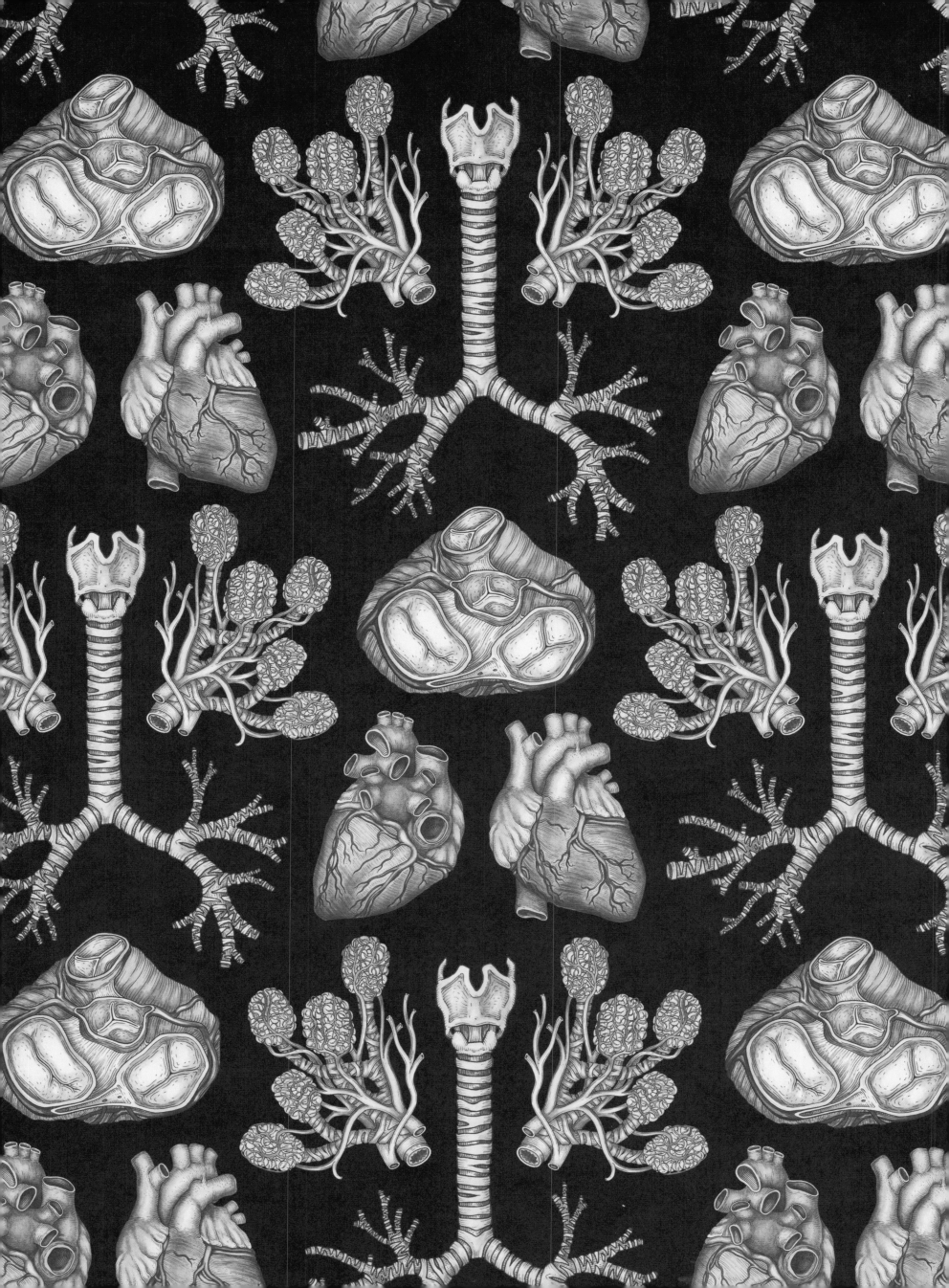

Gallery 2

The Cardiovascular & Respiratory Systems

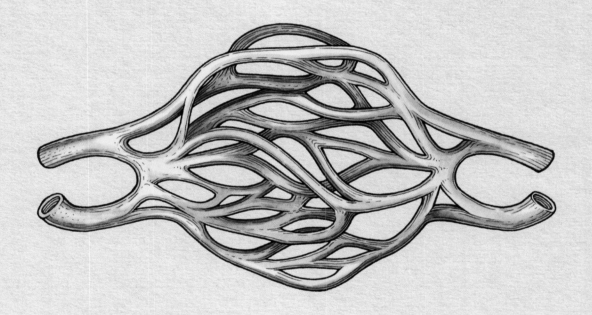

The Cardiovascular & Respiratory Systems

Oxygen is a gas that makes up about 20 percent of the air we breathe. This percentage can fluctuate between temperatures and altitudes, but getting enough into the body is essential to life. Just a few minutes without oxygen can be life-threatening. Every cell in the body needs oxygen to convert into energy—a process known as respiration. When cells release energy, they also produce a gas called carbon dioxide, which the body needs to remove. Inhaling oxygen and exhaling carbon dioxide is the task of the respiratory system. The cardiovascular system is essential in this task. Blood transports oxygen to each and every cell while simultaneously removing carbon dioxide waste.

To reach the body's cells, oxygen has to undertake a long journey through both systems. First, air is inhaled and travels through the trachea, or windpipe, to reach the lungs. Here oxygen is transferred into the body's bloodstream and enters the cardiovascular system. The oxygenated blood then travels throughout the body's vast network of blood vessels, powered onward by the beating of the heart. On arrival at each cell, blood delivers oxygen and other nutrients and carries away waste products, including carbon dioxide. After this exchange, deoxygenated blood travels back to the lungs and respiratory system, where carbon dioxide is passed back into the lungs and breathed out. This vital process continues even as we sleep, pumping over 3,700 gallons/14,000 liters of blood around the body every single day.

Key to plate

1: **Heart**

2: **Arterial system (displayed on the right side of the body)**
The collection of blood vessels called arteries transporting blood away from the heart and to the body tissues
a) Ascending aorta
b) Subclavian artery
c) Brachial artery
d) Radial artery
e) Ulnar artery
f) Descending aorta

g) Common iliac artery
h) Femoral artery
i) Popliteal artery
j) Anterior tibial artery
k) Common carotid artery

3: **Venous system (displayed on the left side of the body)**
The collection of blood vessels called veins transporting blood to the heart
a) Superior vena cava
b) Subclavian vein
c) Basilic vein

d) Medial cubital vein
e) Cephalic vein
f) Inferior vena cava
g) Common iliac vein
h) Femoral vein
i) Popliteal vein
j) Anterior tibial vein
k) Internal jugular vein

4: **Lungs**

5: **Trachea (windpipe)**

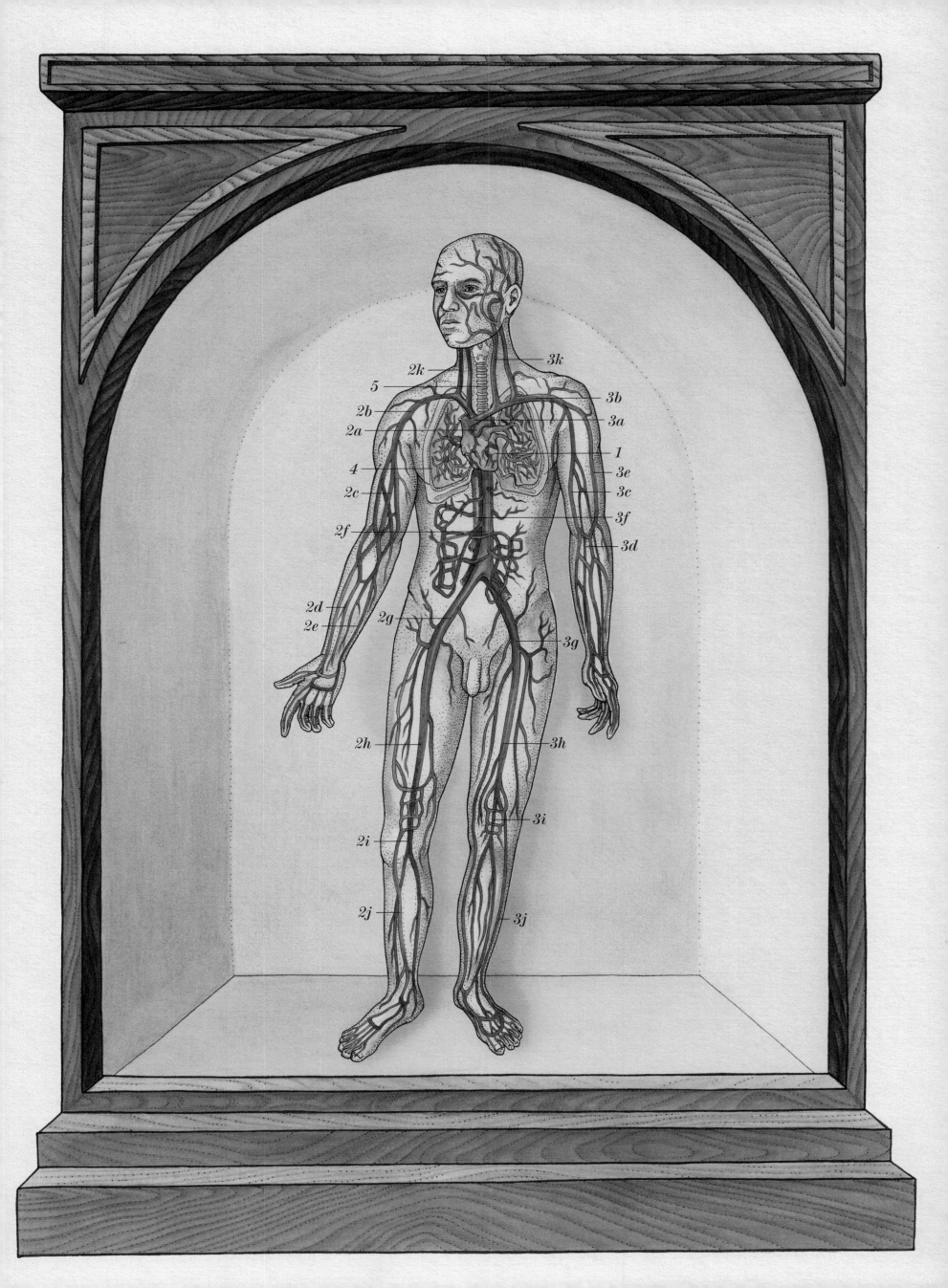

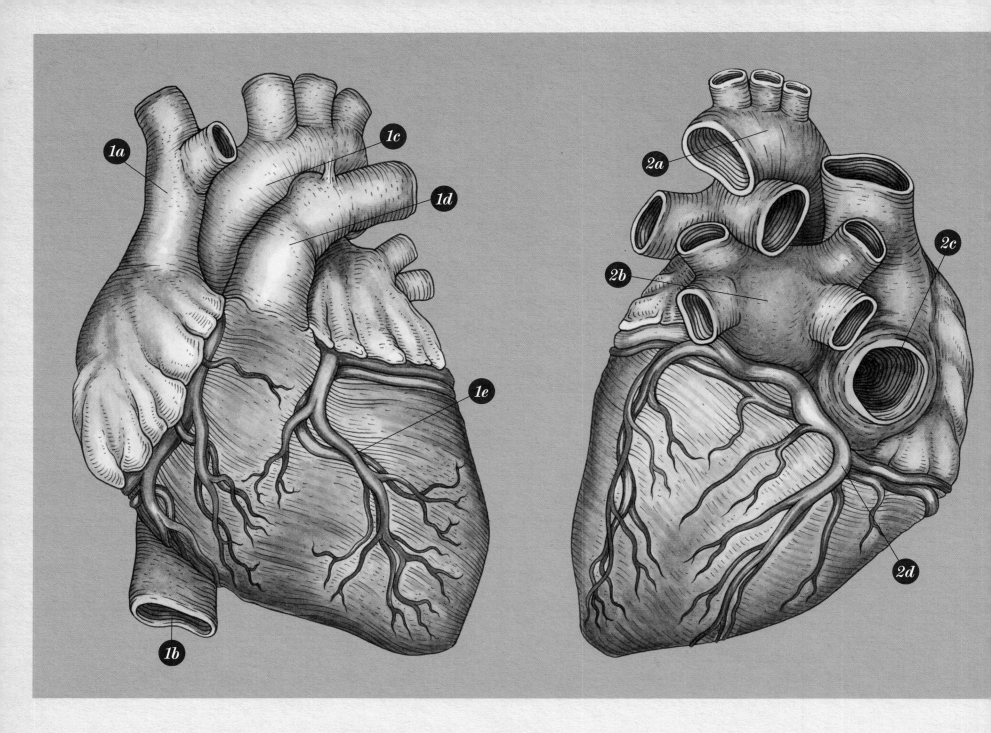

The Heart

The hardest-working muscle in the body is the heart, which beats over 100,000 times every day to transport blood throughout the body. Located under the rib cage and between the lungs, this organ is only about the size of a fist. It acts as a specialized pump—in fact, two pumps in one, each with a vital job to do. The right side of the heart pumps blood toward the lungs, where it picks up oxygen. Oxygen-filled blood returns to the heart, where the left side pumps it on to the rest of the body. A thick wall called the septum divides the right and left sides and keeps the blood separate. Although both sides are similar in appearance, the left side is thicker and stronger, as it has to push blood farther around the body against high pressure.

The pumping action of the heart is produced by cardiac muscle in its walls, which contracts, or squeezes, to push blood between one part of the organ and the other. The four areas, or chambers, within the heart are split into two ventricles at the bottom and two atria at the top. With each heartbeat, the two atria contract first, pushing the blood inside them down into the ventricles. Then the ventricles contract, pushing the blood out of the heart and on to other parts of the body. After contracting, the heart muscle relaxes, allowing the chambers to refill with blood before the next contraction. One complete cycle of this pattern takes less than a second to occur.

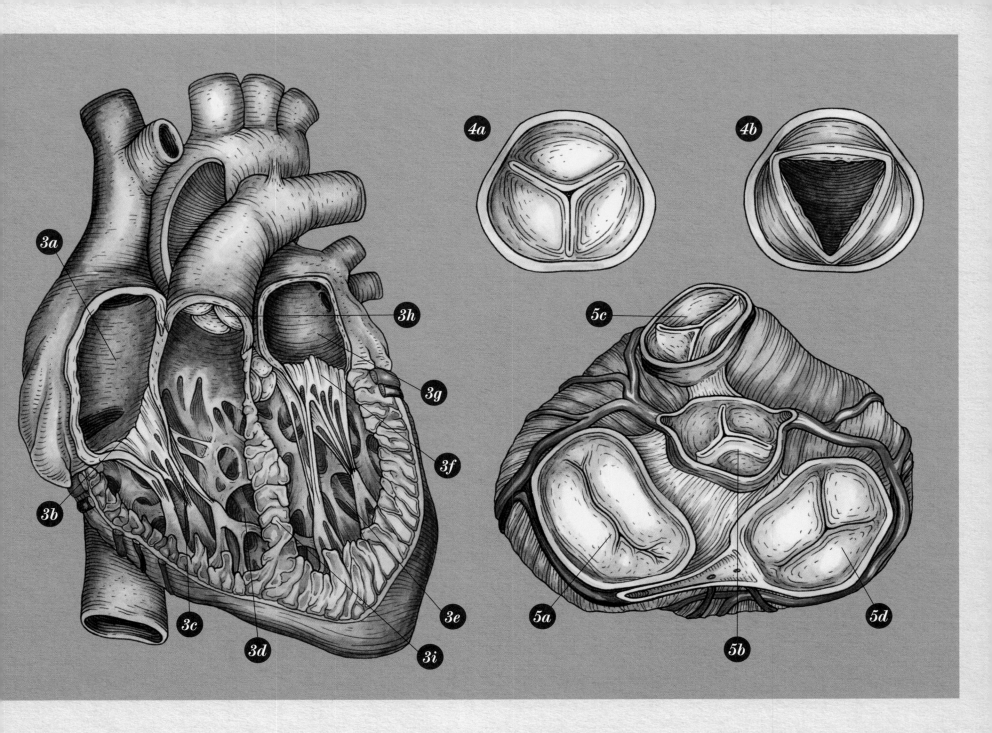

It is crucial that blood only flows in one direction in the heart. To control this, special valves exist in the ventricles, atria, and blood vessels entering and exiting the heart. These act like trapdoors, letting blood flow through one way, but closing tightly to stop it from flowing backward. These valves slamming shut make the rhythmic *lub-dub* sounds of the heart beating.

Key to plate

1: Heart, seen from the front (anterior view)
a) Superior vena cava
b) Inferior vena cava
c) Ascending aorta (to body)
d) Pulmonary trunk (to lungs)
e) Cardiac blood vessels supplying the wall of the heart

2: Heart, seen from behind (posterior view)
a) Arch of aorta
b) Left atrium
c) Entrance to right atrium via inferior vena cava

d) Cardiac vessels draining the wall of the heart

3: Heart, internal structure, from the front (anterior view)
a) Right atrium
b) Tricuspid valve
c) Chordae tendineae (heart strings)
d) Right ventricle
e) Left ventricle
f) Mitral (bicuspid) valve
g) Left atrium
h) Pulmonary valve
i) Interventricular septum

4: Heart valves
Valves between the atria and ventricles, and ventricles and blood vessels, stop blood from flowing backward.
a) Closed
b) Open

5: Heart, with view of the valves, from above (superior view)
a) Mitral (bicuspid) valve
b) Aortic valve
c) Pulmonary valve
d) Tricuspid valve

Blood

Blood is made up of billions of cells, all floating in a liquid called plasma—a watery mix of proteins, salts, nutrients, and hormones. Around 99 percent of blood cells are red. They contain a protein called hemoglobin that binds oxygen molecules to the cell. Hemoglobin also gives blood its red color. By contrast, white blood cells make up only 0.2 percent of blood cells. They patrol the body like an army, attacking infections and removing damaged cells. The rest of the cells in blood are platelets (0.08 percent), which help stop bleeding around cuts. Platelets clot the blood, making it thick and sticky to form a protective scab over the wound site.

A huge network of tubes called blood vessels lets blood travel to every part of our body, from our heads to our toes. Laid end to end, this vascular network would measure over 74,000 miles/120,000 kilometers—long enough to circle the globe three times. Within this network, arteries carry blood away from the heart, veins carry blood toward the heart, and capillaries join the two together.

All blood vessels have walls made of smooth muscle. The thickest walls are in arteries, which must be strong enough to carry high-pressure blood away from the heart. As they move farther from the heart, the arteries divide into arterioles, becoming smaller and smaller like the branches of a tree. When they reach the body's tissues, they become the narrowest type of blood vessel: capillaries. The walls of capillaries are just one cell layer thick, enabling oxygen and carbon dioxide to easily pass between the cells and the blood flow. Once blood has traveled through the capillary, it flows into tiny veins called venules, which get bigger as they get closer to the heart. Veins have much thinner walls than arteries, because the blood they transport is not traveling with so much force. Valves within them ensure blood flows in only one direction and never flows backward. This is especially important in the lower limbs, where deoxygenated blood from the feet needs to be pumped upward, against gravity, back to the heart.

--- *Key to plate* ---

1: **Artery**
These thick-walled tubes transport blood away from the heart. They branch into smaller arterioles before joining capillaries. The biggest artery in the body is the aorta, which is about 1 inch/2–3 centimeters wide and 1 foot/30 centimeters long in adults. It runs directly from the heart into the chest and abdomen.

2: **Capillary bed**
A collection of tiny blood vessels called capillaries form the capillary bed, where gas and nutrient exchange takes place.

3: **Vein**
These muscular tubes have thinner, stretchier walls than arteries and are much wider. They contain valves that stop the backflow of blood as it makes its journey back to the heart.

4: **Blood composition**
a) Plasma: This is a watery mixture of hormones and nutrients that makes blood flowable.

b) Red blood cells: These flat, disc-shaped cells carry oxygen around the body by binding it to hemoglobin, which gives blood its color. Red blood cells are constantly renewed from the bone marrow, only lasting about 120 days in the body before being broken down and removed by the spleen.

c) White blood cells: These are part of the immune system and help the body to fight infection (see page 78).

d) Platelets: These are tiny cells that rush to wounds and form scabs to stop blood from escaping the body.

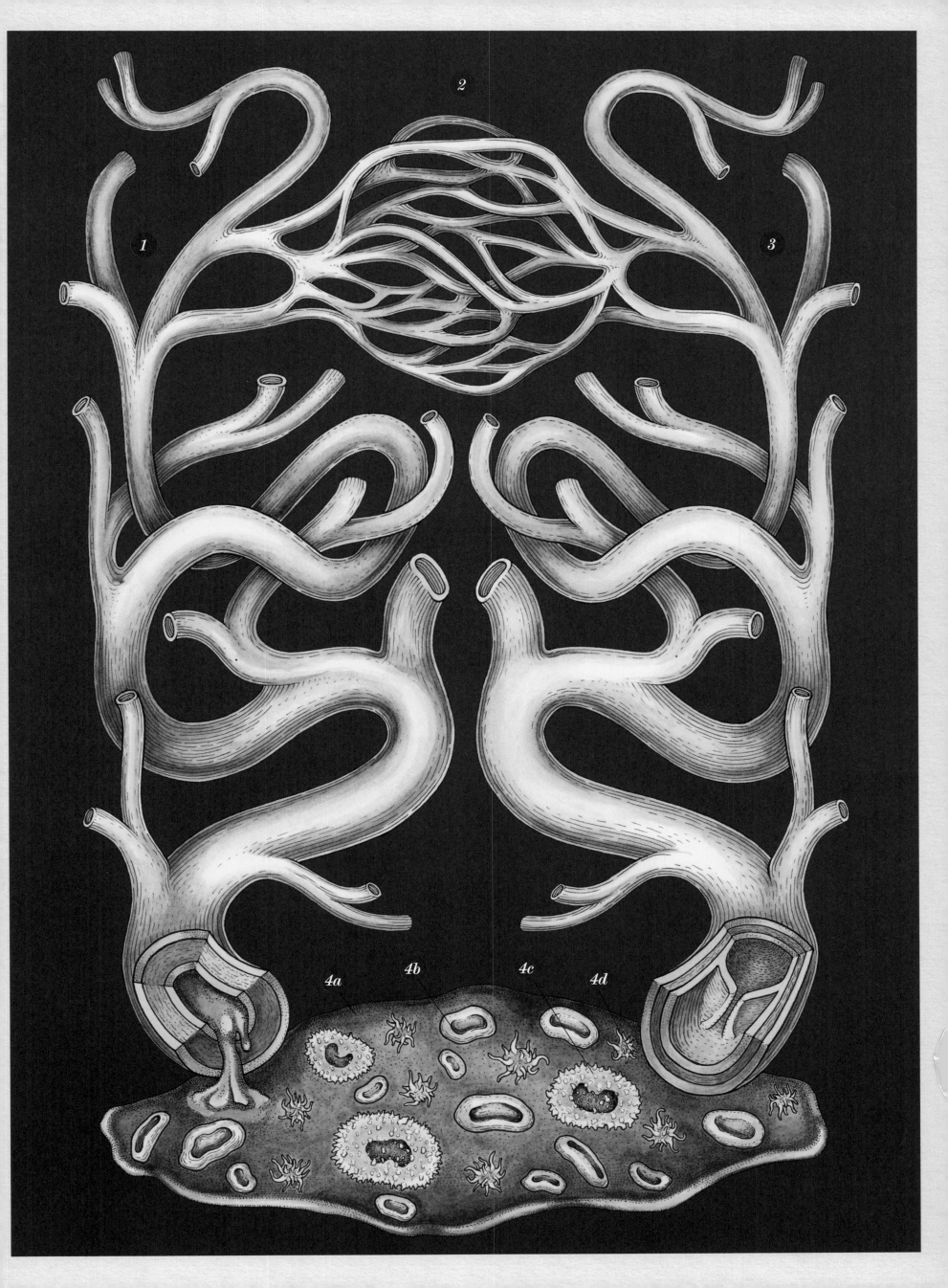

The Respiratory Tract

For the lungs to receive oxygen, air must find its way into the body. This journey begins at the nostrils: two holes in the nose lined with hundreds of little hairs. As air is breathed in, nasal hairs act like filters, trapping dirt and dust particles to stop them from entering the lungs. Once air has passed through the nostrils, it enters the nasal cavity behind the nose, where sticky mucus traps any remaining dust.

From the nasal cavity, air travels through the pharynx, or throat, to the larynx, or voice box, where sound is produced during speech. The larynx contains two small flaps called vocal cords that vibrate when air passes through them. The vocal cords open and close to alter the sounds made when talking, shouting, or singing. Although the mouth and lips form most of the different sounds made when speaking, the larynx is responsible for the volume and pitch of the voice.

After air flows through the larynx, it enters the trachea, or windpipe. The trachea contains rings of cartilage, giving it a ridged appearance and making sure that it is held open to give a clear pathway for air to reach the lungs. At its base, the trachea branches into the bronchi, the two smaller airways that direct air into the lungs.

A major flaw in the human body's design is that food and air both travel along some common routes—the mouth and the throat. When food or drink enters through the mouth, it is normally directed toward the stomach using a clever trapdoor device called the epiglottis. However, if objects enter the windpipe instead, you can start to choke. Coughing, which forces air from the lungs, will usually dislodge an object, but if it isn't removed it can stop air from entering the lungs and even cause death.

Key to plate

1: **Upper respiratory tract, cross section**
a) Nostrils
b) Nasal cavity
c) Pharynx (throat)
d) Larynx (voice box)
e) Vocal cords
f) Sphenoid air sinus

2: **Vocal cords, seen from above (superior view)**
a) Open position: The vocal cords are open during normal breathing, letting air pass through easily.
b) Closed position: The cords close together, allowing a small gap for air to pass through, creating a noise. The tone and volume of the voice change depending on the position of the vocal cords.

3: **The larynx, seen from the front (anterior view)**
a) Hyoid bone: The only bone in the body not attached to another bone, it is instead attached to other structures by membranes.
b) Thyroid cartilage: This looks like a shield and forms the Adam's apple, the protrusion in the neck that is especially prominent in males.
c) Cricoid cartilage: This is joined to the trachea by a membrane.
d) Trachea: Also known as the windpipe, it is held in the shape of an open tube by a series of C-shaped cartilage rings.

4: **The larynx, cross section, seen from behind (posterior view)**
a) Epiglottis: This flap in the throat closes over the larynx during swallowing to stop any food or drink from entering the lungs.
b) Thyroid cartilage
c) Arytenoid cartilages: These protrusions look like two shark fins and help in generating movements of the vocal cords.
d) Cricoid cartilage
e) Trachealis: This muscle constricts the larynx during sneezing or coughing.

5: **Lower respiratory tract**
a) Trachea
b) Carina: The branching point of the trachea into the two primary bronchi
c) Bronchi: Here, the airways enter the lungs, where they begin to branch into smaller and smaller air passages.

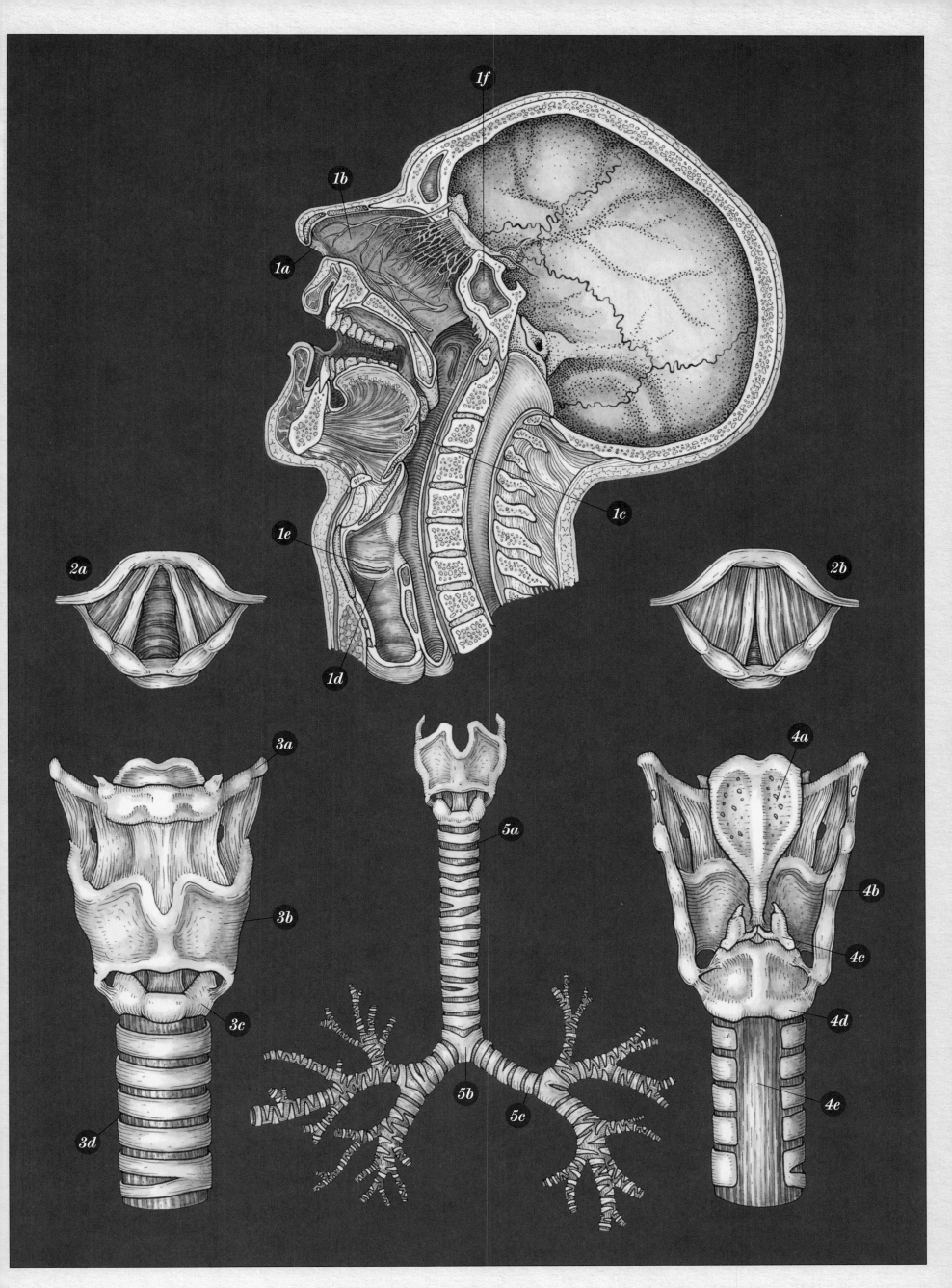

The Lungs

We breathe over 350 cubic feet/10,000 liters of air each day to keep our cells alive and healthy. Getting all of this air in and out of the body is the responsibility of the lungs. These paired organs inhale and exhale air at a rate of around fifteen breaths a minute, transferring oxygen from inhaled air into the bloodstream while passing carbon dioxide from the bloodstream into the air to be exhaled.

Once air enters the lungs, it begins a journey through a dividing network of more tubes that become smaller and smaller as they travel deeper into the organ. Eventually, the air reaches tiny closed sacs called alveoli, which resemble small bunches of grapes. Each individual alveolus (singular of alveoli) is covered in a tiny blood vessel called a capillary (see page 32). The walls of the alveoli and the capillaries are only one cell layer thick (less than a thousandth of a millimeter), so gases can easily be exchanged to and from the blood. There are several hundred million alveoli in an adult's lungs, meaning they have a huge surface area that allows gas to transfer quickly. In fact, the total surface area of the lungs is estimated to be bigger than that of a tennis court!

The right and left lungs sit within the chest, under the rib cage. The right lung has three different parts, or lobes, and is a little bigger than the left, which has only two lobes. The left lung is smaller to make room for the heart that fits snugly between the two lungs. A large, dome-shaped muscle called the diaphragm is found directly underneath the lungs, separating them from the organs in the abdomen. The diaphragm helps to create space in the chest when we breathe in, or inhale, by pulling downward and flattening out. This lets the lungs fill with air, inflating like balloons and raising the rib cage outward. When we breathe out, or exhale, the diaphragm relaxes and pushes on the lungs, squeezing the air back out again. This cycle happens between twelve and twenty times each minute when resting, and much more often during exercise as breathing rate increases.

───────────────── *Key to plate* ─────────────────

1: **Lungs**
a) Trachea
b) Bronchi
c) Bronchioles
d) Pleural membranes: Two thin, fluid-filled membranes encase the lungs and enable them to move smoothly as they inflate and deflate.
e) Right lung
f) Left lung

2: **Alveoli**
a) Venule
b) Arteriole
c) Capillary bed
The millions of alveoli in each lung group together to form small bunches. Tiny capillaries wrap around them so that gas can easily transfer between the blood and the air in the alveoli.

3: **Cross section of alveoli**
Inside each grapelike cluster are dozens of individual alveoli. Each one has a wall just one cell layer thick so oxygen can easily enter the bloodstream.

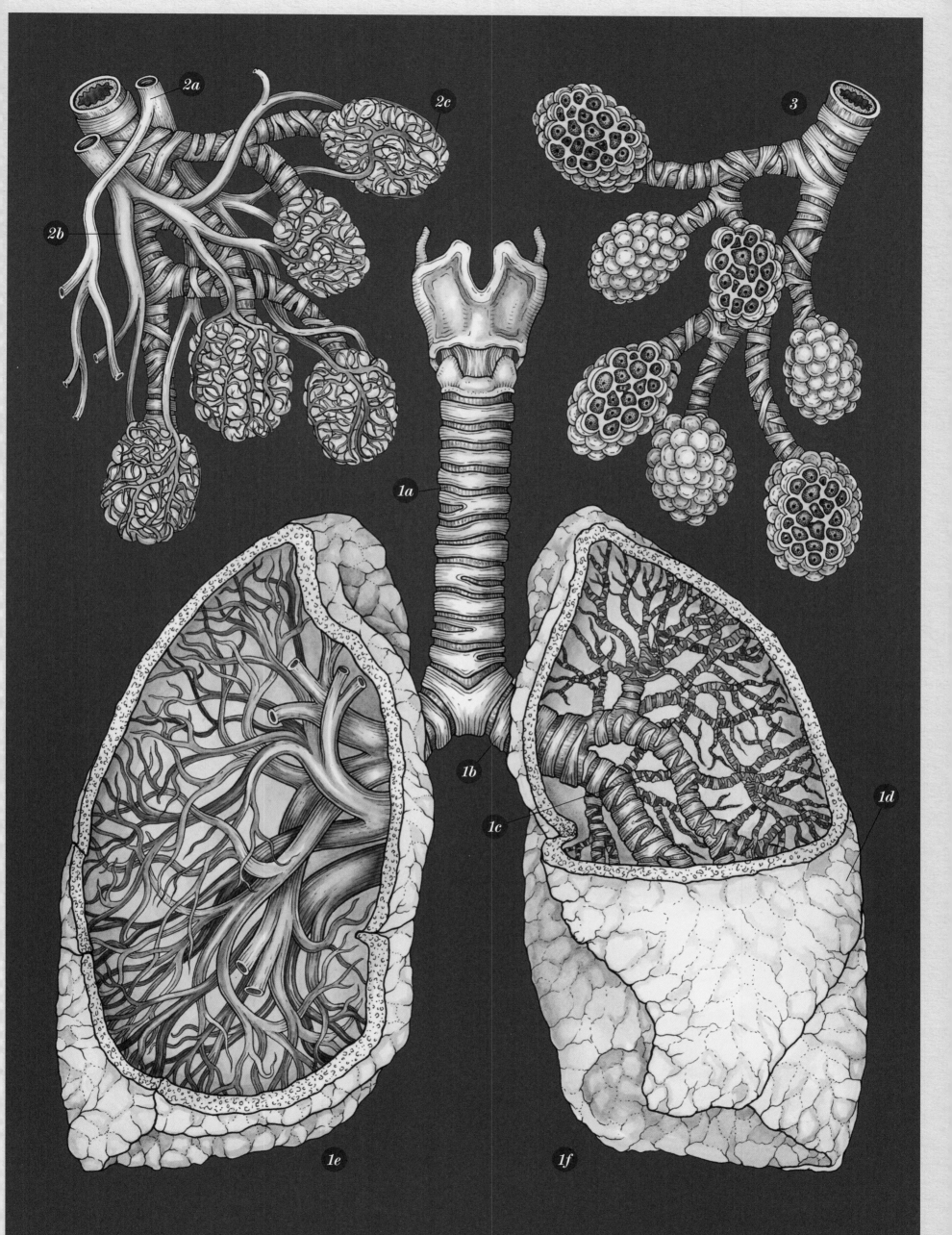

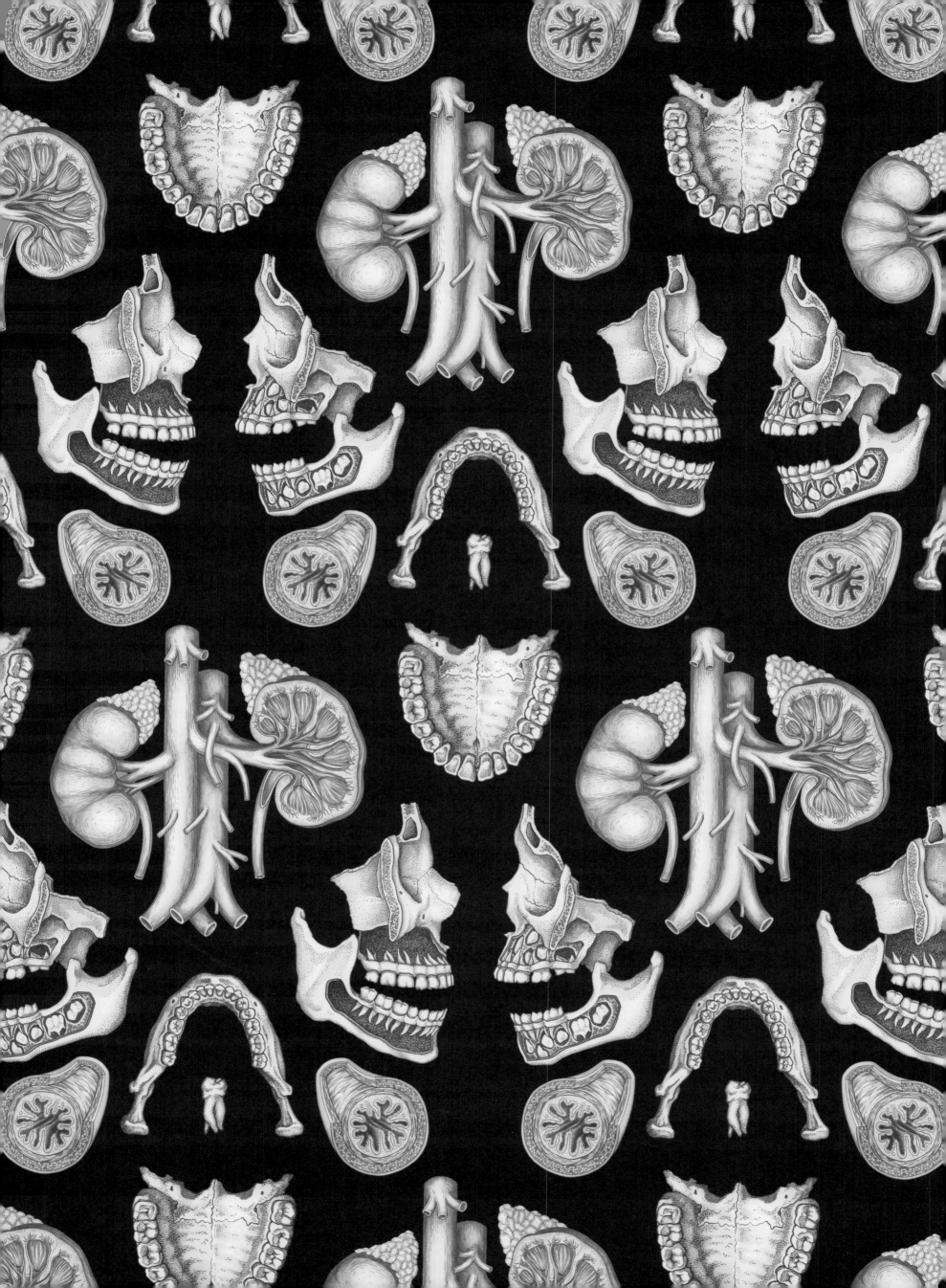

Gallery 3

The Digestive & Urinary Systems

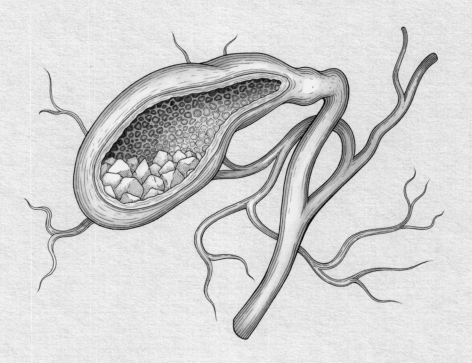

The Digestive System

The digestive system is a clever food-processing plant, working constantly to take in food, break it down into the nutrients we need, and get rid of the waste that's left. The main part of the system is the digestive tract—23 feet/7 meters of long, muscular tubes, most of which are squashed into the body's abdomen. It is made of seven interconnected organs, which effectively form a direct path all the way from the mouth to the anus.

Food enters the body via the mouth, where it is chewed and swallowed. Then it passes through the pharynx, or throat, and into the esophagus, or food pipe, on its way to the stomach. There, food is broken down into a thick, soup-like liquid before being passed into the small intestine and then the large intestine. The intestines are where essential nutrients are absorbed into the bloodstream. Once in the large intestine, the waste material forms feces and leaves the body through the rectum and anus.

The process of breaking down food to generate energy is known as digestion. Its main task is to turn complex food molecules into smaller ones the body can use. First of all, food is digested mechanically: broken down into physically smaller chunks, initially by chewing in the mouth, then by churning and mixing using the muscles of the stomach. Food is also digested chemically: special molecules called enzymes, which are found in saliva in the mouth and released as a liquid into the stomach and intestines, break nutrients such as fats, proteins, and carbohydrates into even smaller parts such as amino acids, used for building new molecules, and glucose, used for energy.

Although the digestive tract is the main path that food takes through the body, it does not work alone: the liver, gallbladder, and pancreas all aid digestion by releasing special chemicals into it. Controlling all the complex processes of eating, digestion, and excretion are a combination of nerve signals and hormones. Emotions can affect the digestive system, too, as you will know if you have ever felt the sensation of "butterflies in your stomach" when you are nervous, or if you have felt sick with excitement.

Key to plate

1: **The mouth (oral cavity)**
The opening to the digestive system, where food and drink enter the body

2: **The pharynx (throat)**
This connects the mouth to the esophagus.

3: **The esophagus**
A long, muscular tube that connects the pharynx to the stomach

4: **The stomach**
A large, muscular bag that stores and digests food

5: **The small intestine**
This long passageway joins the stomach to the large intestine. Digested food is passed through the small intestine, where the nutrients it contains are absorbed into the body's bloodstream.

6: **The large intestine**
The waste products of digested food pass through the large intestine, where any remaining water is absorbed back into the bloodstream. The remaining dry waste then passes to the rectum and anus, where it will exit the body.

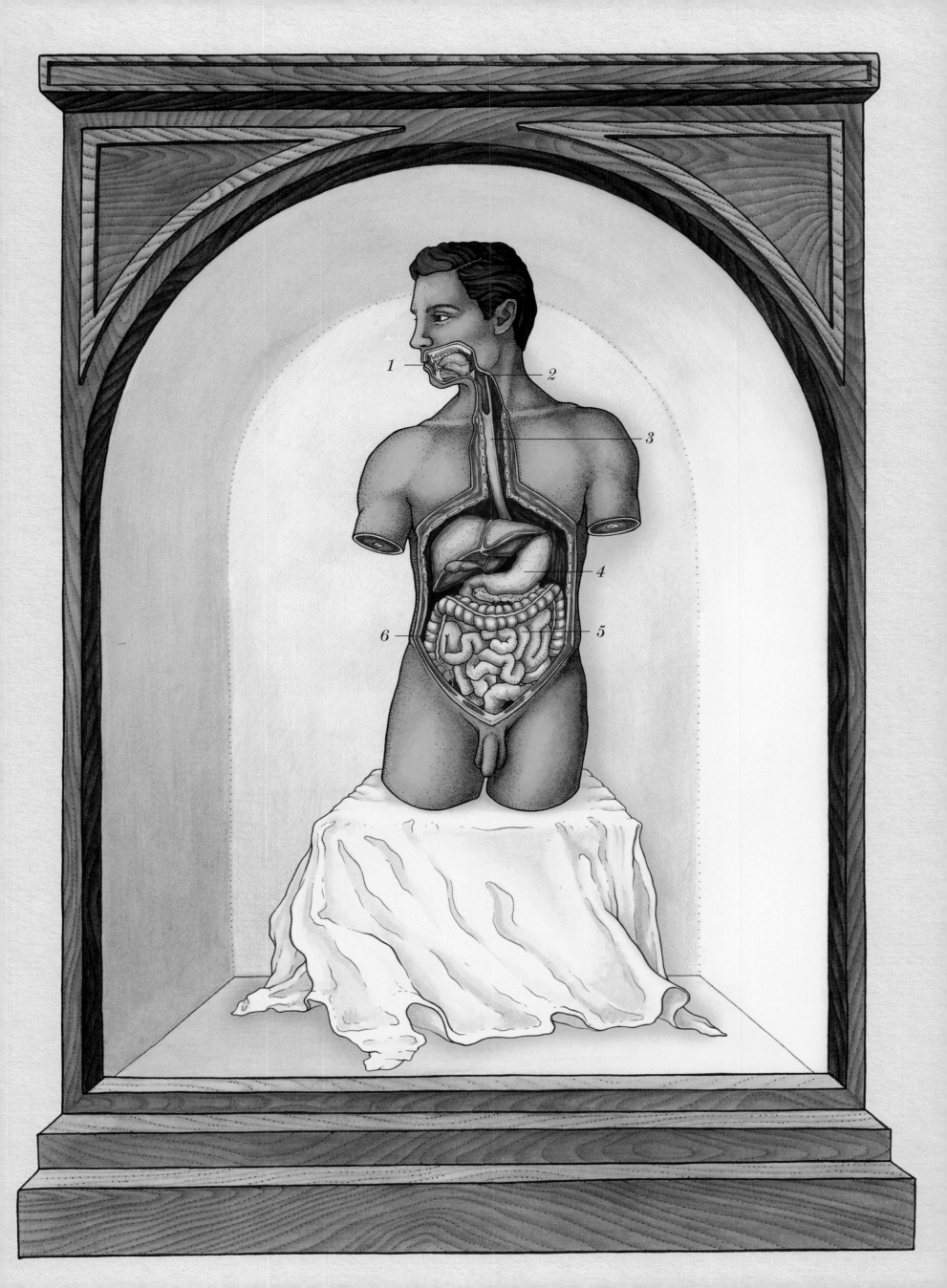

The Mouth
& Throat

The oral cavity, known as the mouth, is the gateway to the body: this is where all food and drink starts its journey through the digestive system. Even before you take your first bite of food, your body begins to prepare itself for digestion. The smell of food cooking, or sometimes just the thought of a tasty meal, is enough to kick-start the salivary glands into action. They pump out a watery liquid called saliva—on average over 1/2 gallon/2 liters each day—literally making your mouth water. As well as making the food you eat wetter and easier to swallow, saliva contains chemicals called enzymes, which start to break down complex molecules within food. Teeth also grind food down mechanically, and, together with the tongue, help shape food into a ball called a bolus, which is easy to swallow.

At the moment of swallowing, an important safety mechanism kicks in at the top of the pharynx, or throat. A small trapdoor called the epiglottis swings into place, covering the entrance to the trachea, or windpipe, as food and drink slips into the esophagus. This ensures no food or drink accidentally enters the respiratory system. Sometimes the epiglottis fails and things go down the wrong way—but a cough is usually enough to clear the airway again, and no harm is done.

Once a food bolus has passed the epiglottis, it travels down the esophagus, a long, muscular tube. Rather than acting as an open chute that food simply falls down, the muscles of the esophagus squeeze the bolus down toward the stomach. Incredibly, this means food would still reach the stomach even if you were standing on your head!

Key to plate

1: **The mouth (oral cavity)**
a) Teeth: The thirty-two teeth are used to rip, tear, and grind food into smaller pieces that can be swallowed.
b) Tongue: This organ is made up of several muscles, the largest of which is the genioglossus. During swallowing, the tongue shapes the food and pushes it toward the back of the mouth.

2: **The pharynx (throat)**
a) Food bolus
b) Epiglottis: Although it is usually classified as part of the respiratory system, the epiglottis has an important role in the digestive system. During swallowing, it folds over the larynx, stopping food from entering the airway.

3: **The esophagus**
This muscular tube, approximately 10 inches/25 centimeters long, runs from the pharynx to the stomach, transporting the food bolus on into the rest of the digestive system.

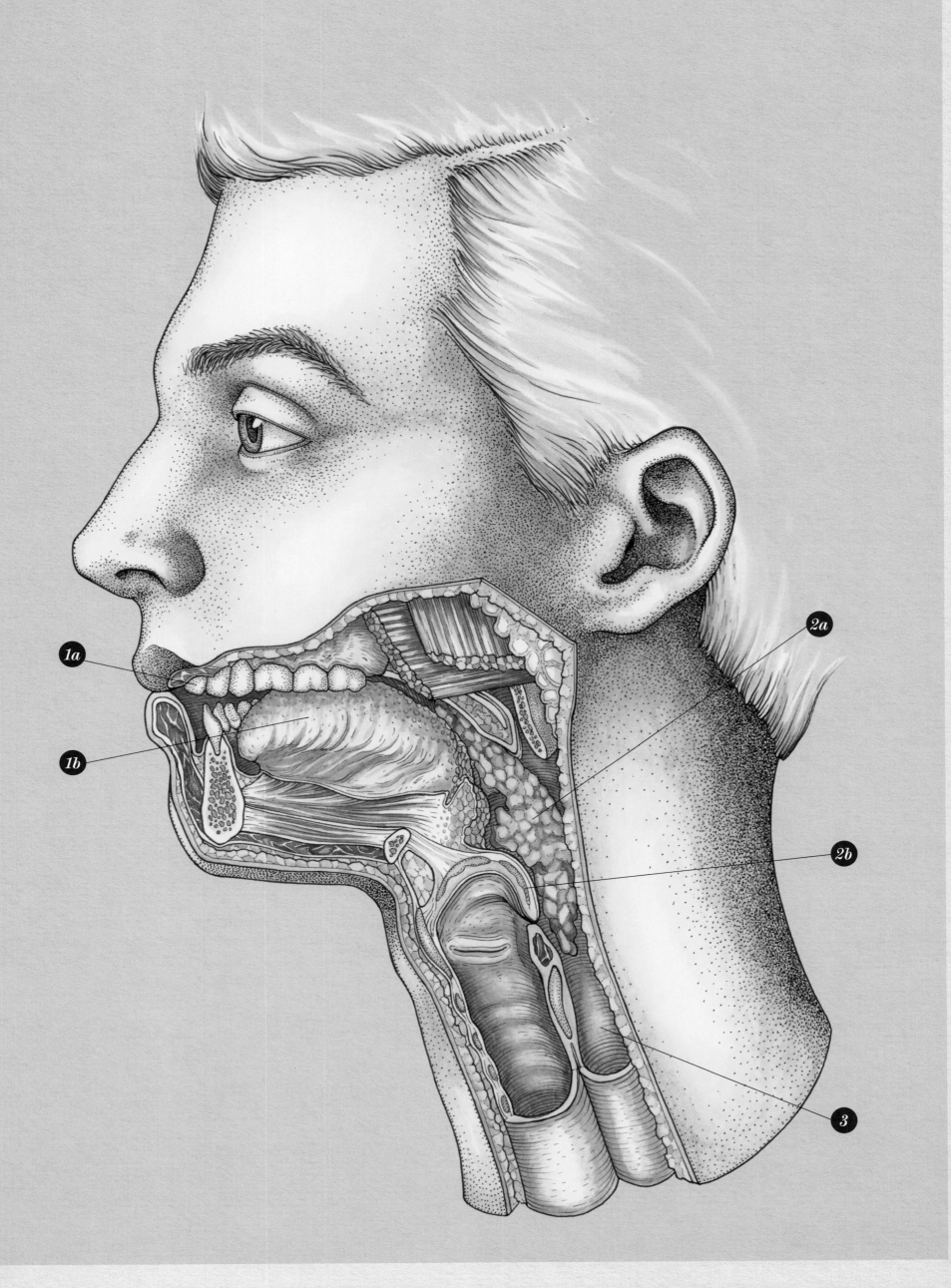

The Teeth

The adult mouth contains thirty-two teeth, arranged in two neat rows across the upper and lower jaws. Their job is to make food soft, smooth, and suitable for swallowing.

Babies are usually born without any teeth at all, and the first tooth will push through the gums when a child is around six months old. Slowly, the teeth emerge into the mouth, and children have a full set of twenty "baby teeth" or "milk teeth" by around three years of age. As children grow up, the baby teeth start to be pushed out by permanent adult teeth that lie in the jaws behind them. By the time most people enter their thirties, they have thirty-two teeth in total, including four wisdom teeth at the very back of the mouth that only start coming through in the teenage years, though sometimes these are removed. This final set of adult teeth needs to last for an entire lifetime, since teeth cannot repair themselves. Holes, called cavities, can appear in the teeth due to decay, and these need to be repaired by a dentist. If the decay is too severe or a tooth is damaged by trauma, the whole tooth is sometimes removed.

The shape of a tooth and its position within the mouth are good indicators of their function. At the front of the mouth are the incisors: sharp, thin teeth that easily slice into food. Next to the incisors are the canines, more pointed in shape and also used to bite, tear, or hold food. Premolars and molars, which sit at the back of the mouth, have a flat, squarish shape with ridges on their top surface. The molars especially are ideally shaped to crush and grind food during chewing.

Each tooth is made up of several layers. The outer layer of enamel acts like a protective armor encasing the crown (top) of the tooth and gives teeth their whitish color due to its high levels of minerals such as calcium. Underneath the enamel lies the dentine, a hard substance that protects the dental pulp in the center of the tooth—a soft cushioning around the tooth's sensitive blood vessels and nerves. The bottom part of the tooth, the root, sits buried deep into the gums overlying the jawbone. Individual teeth are anchored into the jaw by fibrous joints covered in a layer of cementum. As the name suggests, this substance keeps the tooth firmly cemented in place.

Key to plate

1: **Adult's skull**
The roots of the teeth reach deep into the jaw bones.

2: **Child's skull**
Here we can see the permanent teeth developing behind the milk teeth. They push into the mouth during childhood, loosening and eventually pushing out the milk teeth.

3: **Types of adult teeth**
a) Molars (12): The molars, including wisdom teeth, which appear during adulthood, have flat, wide surfaces shaped to grind and mash food.
b) Premolars (8): Smaller in size than the molars, these also grind food.
c) Canines (4): There is one canine on the upper and lower jaws at each side. We use these sharp, pointed teeth to bite and tear food.
d) Incisors (8): There are four incisors on both the upper and lower jaw. Their flat, thin shape acts like a knife, slicing food.

4: **Upper jaw (maxilla), from below (inferior view)**

5: **Lower jaw (mandible), from above (superior view)**

6: **Structure of a tooth**
a) Enamel: A tooth's hard outer layer
b) Dentine: This lies beneath the enamel.
c) Pulp: Soft dental pulp lies within the center of the tooth and contains blood vessels, cells, and nerves.
d) Root: The root is the part of the tooth secured into the gums.
e) Cementum: This hard substance surrounds the root of the tooth and secures it in place in the jaw.

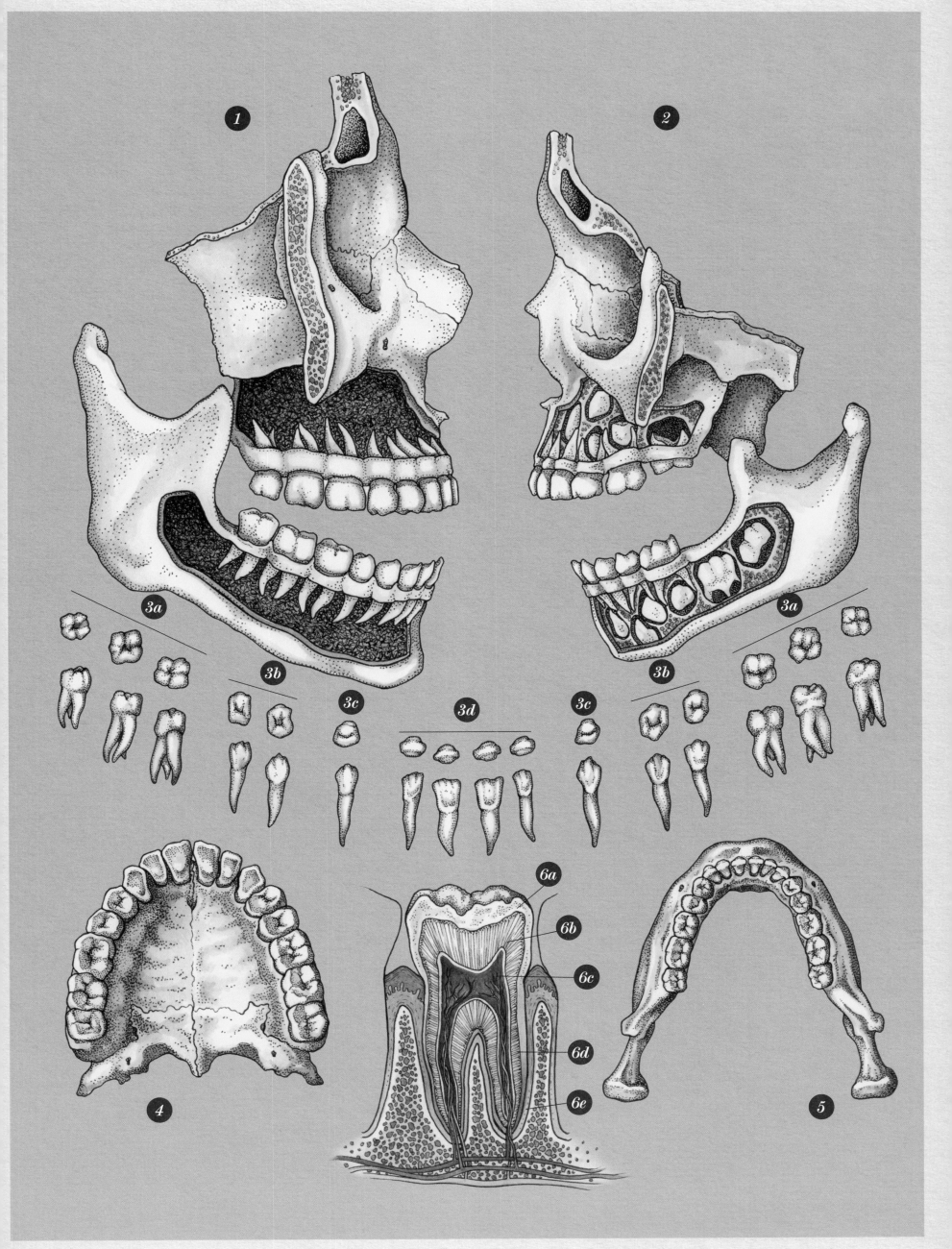

The Stomach

After food has been swallowed, it is transported to the stomach: a curved, muscular bag in the upper left region of the abdomen. The stomach stores the food we eat while vigorously churning to mix it with stomach acid. Then the resulting mixture — a thick, soupy mix called chyme — is passed on to the next part of the digestive tract.

About 3 pints/1.5 liters of stomach acid, or gastric juice, is produced by cells in the stomach lining every day. It chemically digests food by breaking down long molecules into smaller ones (see page 40). It also helps to kill any dangerous bacteria present in the food. A layer of mucus on the stomach lining stops the wall of the stomach from being damaged by the acidic juice. Occasionally an infection might stop mucus production, in which case the acid starts to eat away at the stomach, producing a hole called an ulcer. These are painful.

The walls of the stomach are made from smooth muscle, arranged into three separate layers. The fibers in these overlapping muscle layers run in different directions: from left to right, top to bottom, and diagonally around the stomach walls. This means that when they contract, the stomach moves in a churning or mixing motion, helping to blend the chyme. Have you ever heard your stomach "rumble" when you haven't eaten for a while? This is just the normal sound of the movement of the stomach as it churns. When the stomach is empty, it fills with gas, and without any food to muffle the noise, the growling sounds much louder. At its fullest, an adult stomach can hold approximately 2 to 4 pints/1 to 2 liters of food and drink. To cope with the need to expand, the inside walls of the stomach are folded into numerous ridges that fan out, stretching the walls as the stomach fills up. Special sensors in the stomach wall can tell if the stomach is stretched, giving you a feeling of fullness.

Food can stay in the stomach for as little as twenty minutes or for many hours, depending on what has been eaten and based on the individual. Simple foods like cooked fruits and vegetables will be digested fairly quickly, but rich, greasy foods may take several hours. Once the chyme is ready to leave the stomach, a special valve at its base will let small amounts through to the small intestine, carefully controlling the speed at which the food makes its journey through the body.

Key to plate

1: **Esophagus**
The muscular tube leading from the pharynx (throat) to the stomach

2: **Cardiac sphincter**
This ring of smooth muscle acts like a valve to let food into the stomach while preventing food and stomach acid from traveling back up into the esophagus.

3: **Layers of the stomach wall**
a) Oblique muscles
b) Circular muscles
c) Longitudinal muscles

4: **Stomach**
The inner surface of this muscular bag has thick folds, called rugae. These stretch as the stomach fills and allow the stomach to expand in size.

5: **Pyloric sphincter**
This ring of smooth muscle ensures the controlled release of chyme from the stomach to the small intestine and prevents the backflow of chyme into the stomach.

6: **Duodenum**
This is the first portion of the small intestine.

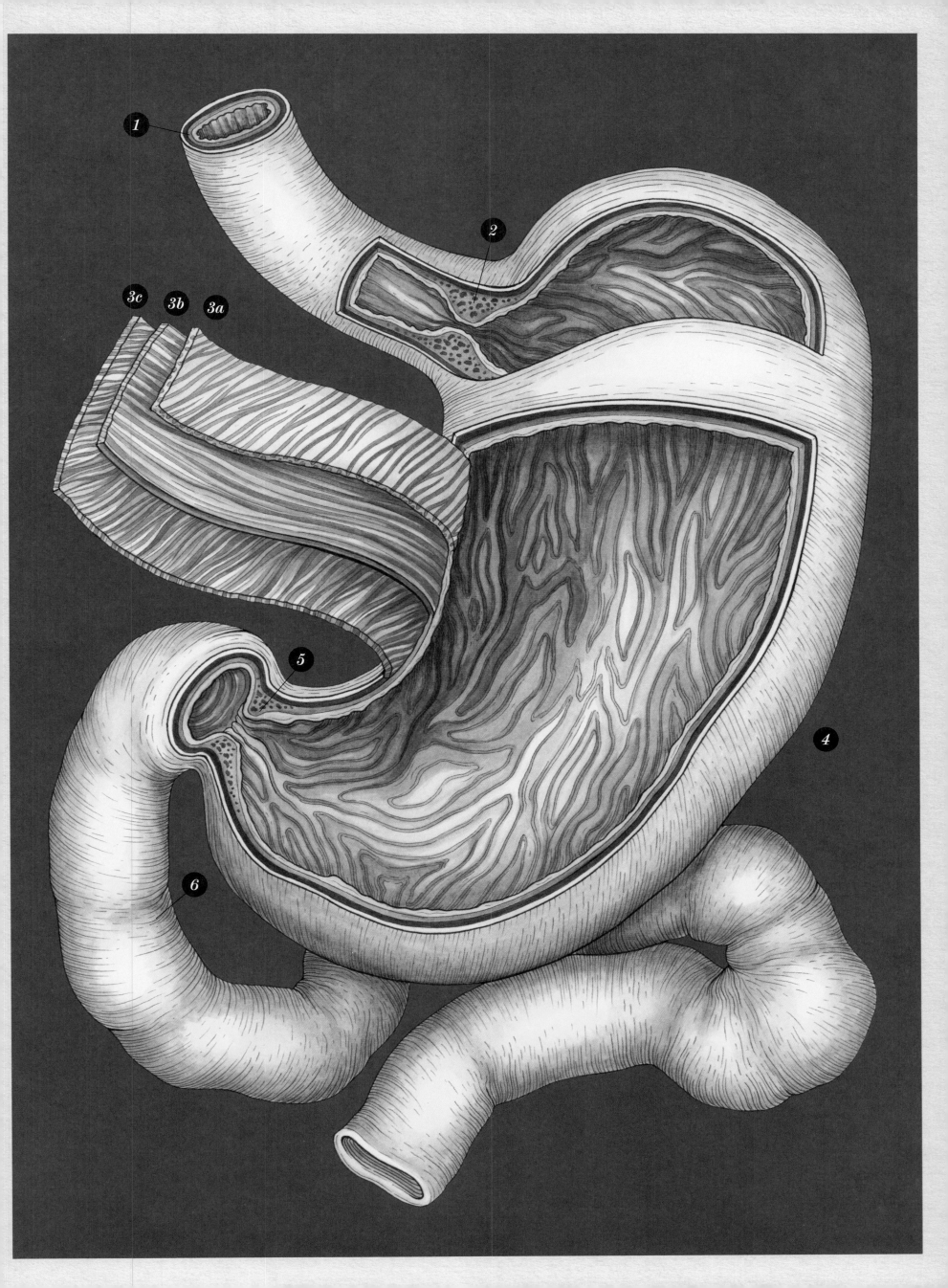

The Intestines

The long tubes of the small and large intestines are where the main process of digestion and absorption takes place (see page 40). The terms "small" and "large" refer to the width of the intestines rather than their length; in fact, the small intestine is actually the longest part of the digestive system. Beginning at the exit of the stomach, the small intestine is made of three parts: the duodenum, the jejunum, and the ileum. The short, curved duodenum is where acidic chyme from the stomach meets alkaline fluids secreted by the liver, gallbladder, and pancreas, reducing the acidity of the chyme and making sure that the intestine's digestive enzymes can work properly. After this, chyme is propelled along the loops and coils of the jejunum and ileum by regular waves of muscle contractions called peristalsis. Along the way, the chyme continues to be digested and absorbed.

Aside from being very long, the walls of the small intestine are tightly folded and covered with millions of tiny finger-like projections called villi. Together, these hugely increase the surface area of the intestines—stretched out, they would cover an area of about 2,700 square feet/250 square meters. The large surface area facilitates the absorption of nutrients and water, which pass straight into the blood vessels within the villi.

Once chyme reaches the large intestine, or colon, the body has already absorbed most of the nutrients it contains, leaving behind a mix of water and waste material to be disposed of. As the chyme is pushed through the 5 feet/1.5 meters of large intestine, its water content is absorbed back into the body. This process can take a long time (up to forty hours), but it is essential to dry out the chyme and make solid waste called feces. Feces is stored in the rectum until it exits the body through the anus.

Key to plate

1: **Small intestine, surface view**
The long tube where most nutrients are absorbed during digestion. It is split into the duodenum, jejunum, and ileum, though these parts are hard to distinguish by appearance alone.

2: **Large intestine, surface view**
This is where water is absorbed from food waste before it leaves the body. The puckerings of the large intestine are called haustra.
a) Rectum: The part of the large intestine where feces is stored

b) Anus: The exit point of the large intestine, where feces leaves the body
c) Taenia coli: A line of muscle visible on the outside of the large intestine

3: **Cross section of small intestine**
a) Inner mucosa: Its folded surface lined with villi gives this layer a high surface area for increased absorption.
b) Submucosa: Carries blood vessels, nerves, and lymphatic vessels.
c) Muscular layers: Two connecting layers of muscle contract to propel food along the digestive tract.

d) Outer covering (serosa): A connective tissue coating

4: **Villi of the small intestine**
Finger-like projections called villi line the small intestine, increasing its surface area so nutrients can quickly be absorbed into the bloodstream.
a) Epithelial layer: This top layer is just one cell thick.
b) Blood and lymphatic vessels (see page 76)

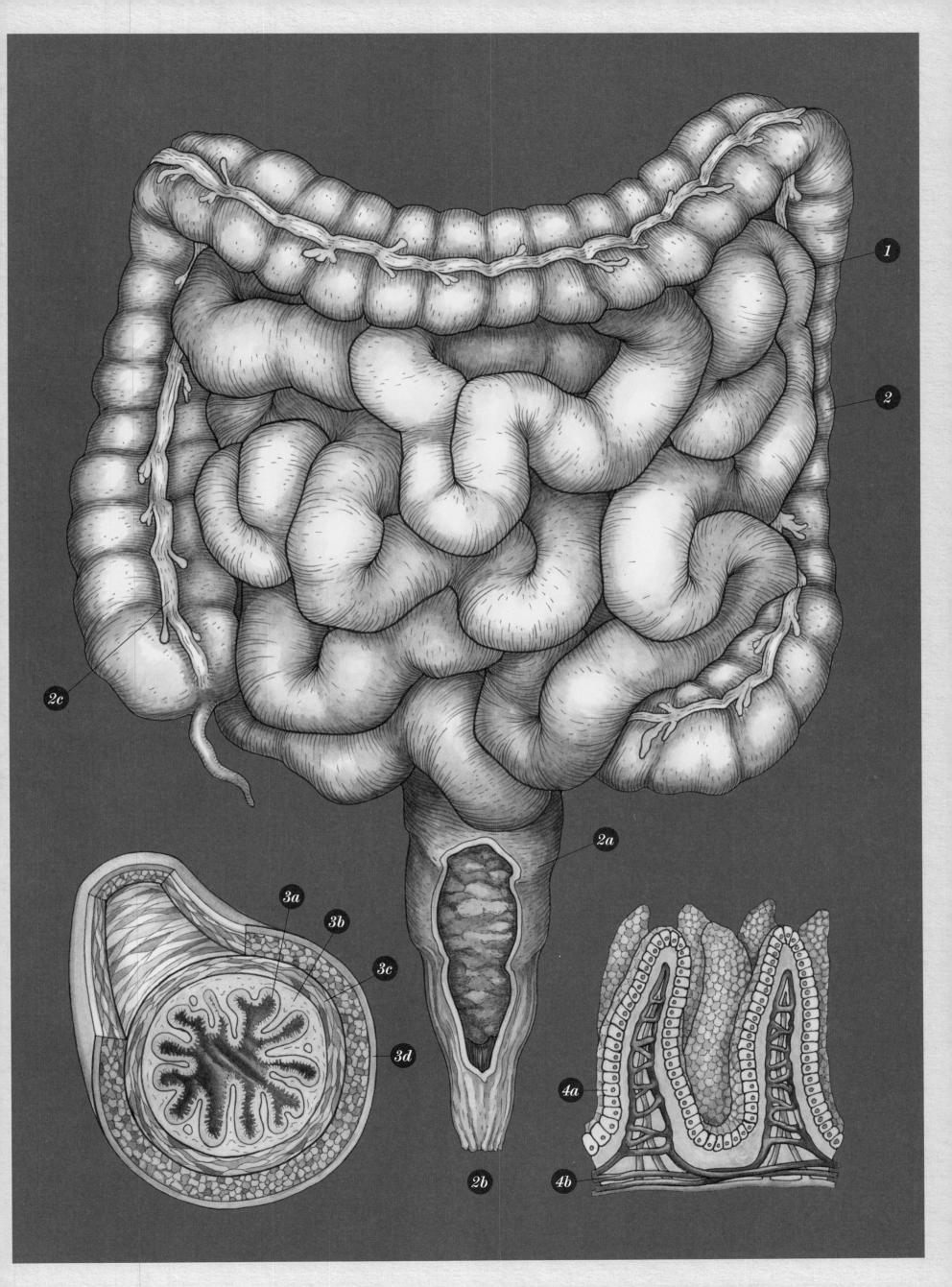

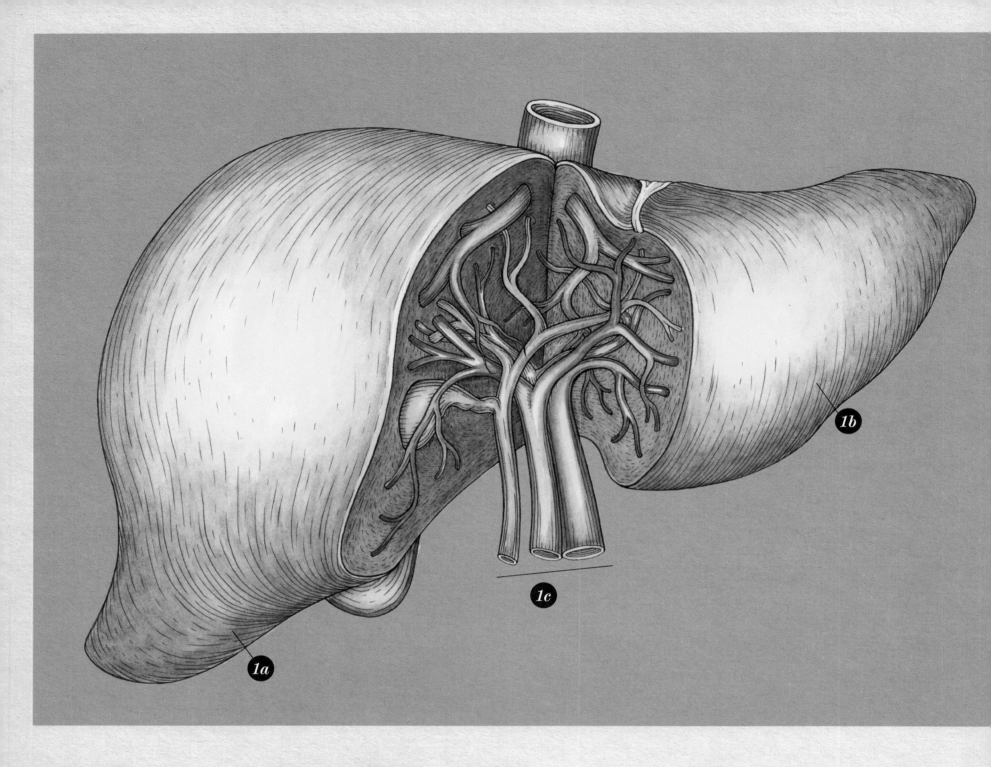

The Liver

The liver carefully orchestrates hundreds of processes to keep the blood clean and the body healthy. The largest organ inside the body, it sits in the upper right region of the abdomen, just under the rib cage and diaphragm. It is roughly triangular in shape with four different parts, or lobes, and is a deep red color because of its extensive blood supply. Indeed, the liver receives over 10 percent of all the blood in the body at any one time and pumps an astonishing 3 pints/1.5 liters of blood through it every minute.

The liver serves three major roles: cleaning the blood, producing bile, and storing energy. First, the liver cleans the blood, removing any substances that might be harmful. These can be leftover products of food after digestion or toxic substances such as certain medicines or alcohol. Often, the liver can change toxic substances into molecules that are less harmful to the body. Otherwise, it sends the toxic substances via the digestive system to exit the body in feces, or via the kidneys to leave the body in urine. Second, the liver makes bile: a thick yellow-green liquid that is needed to help the body digest fat. Bile is either released into the small intestine right away or sent to the gallbladder to be stored until it's needed. Third, the liver stores and produces energy, like a battery that charges and bursts into action when energy levels are low. The liver is "charged" by blood coming from the small and large intestines, packed full of the nutrients absorbed during digestion.

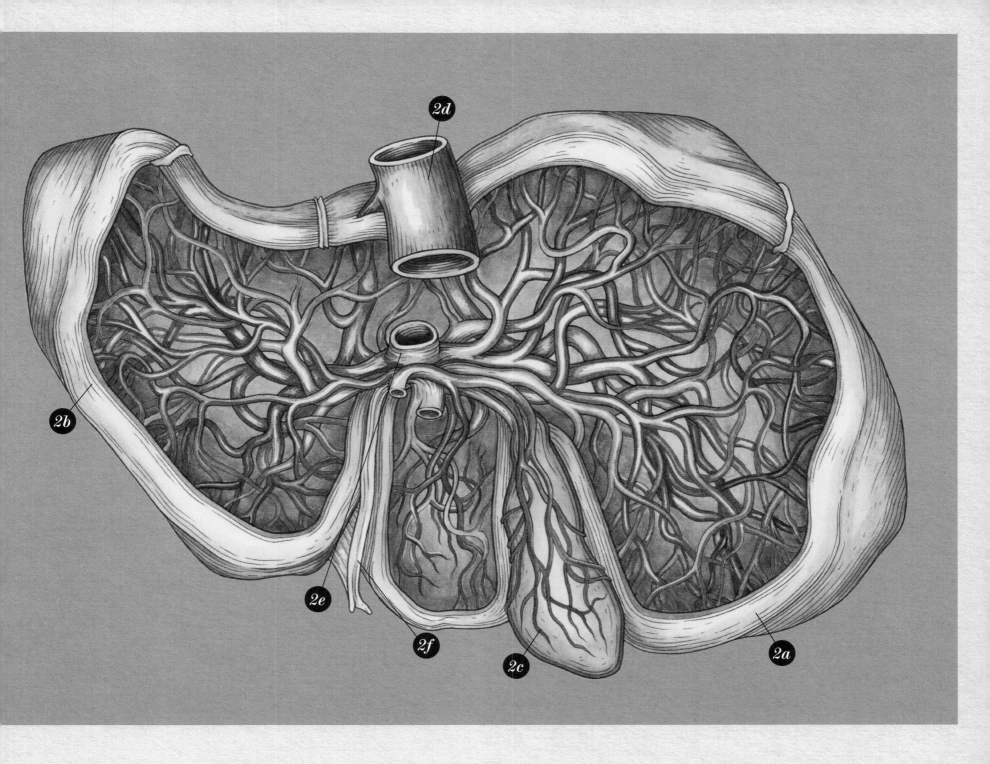

From the intestines, the blood is directed via the liver through a special set of blood vessels known as the hepatic portal system. Any toxic substances in this blood will also reach the liver this way, to be filtered out and removed from the body.

Interestingly, the liver has an amazing feature shared by no other organ in the human body: it can regenerate. Damage to the liver, caused by disease or too much alcohol, can stop it from working properly and make a person very ill. However, if the damaged parts of the liver are removed (leaving at least a third behind), the rest of the liver can actually grow back and become full size again.

Key to plate

1: Liver, seen from the front (anterior view)
a) Right lobe
b) Left lobe
c) Hepatic portal system: Blood travels to the liver from the small and large intestines (where it becomes rich in nutrients). Oxygen-rich blood also arrives at the liver from the main blood supply of the abdomen. Meanwhile, bile made in the liver is transported through here to the gallbladder for storage, or straight to the small intestine.

2: Liver, seen from behind (posterior view)
The liver has a very extensive blood supply.
a) Left lobe
b) Right lobe
c) Gallbladder

d) Inferior vena cava: Blood leaving the liver exits here on its way back to the heart.
e) Hepatic portal vein: Blood coming from the intestines enters the liver here.
f) Falciform ligament: This connective tissue structure divides the liver into left and right lobes. It also helps to attach the liver to the inside of the abdomen.

The Pancreas
& Gallbladder

The pancreas has an important role to play both in the digestive system and the endocrine system (see page 82). Leaf-shaped and uniquely textured, it lies near the stomach, with its head nesting snugly into the curve of the duodenum (the first part of the small intestine). This position enables it to release pancreatic juice directly into the intestines, neutralizing acidic chyme before it travels any farther through the digestive system.

When a gland releases a substance straight into an organ or tissue like this, it is known as an exocrine function. The pancreas is a special gland as it also has an endocrine function, meaning it releases chemicals directly into the blood as well. Two of the chemicals produced by the pancreas are insulin and glucagon, which are important hormones for controlling sugar levels. If levels are low, you might feel dizzy or light-headed; then the pancreas produces glucagon to tell the liver to release sugar. If your sugar levels are too high, the pancreas produces insulin, which reduces the amount of sugar in the blood. Sometimes, the pancreas stops producing these hormones in a condition called diabetes, and insulin injections are needed to help control sugar levels.

The point where pancreatic juice enters into the small intestine is also the entrance for another liquid crucial for digestion: bile. Bile is made in the liver but stored in a small muscular bag called the gallbladder. Although it is mostly made from water, bile also contains lots of salts and fats, which in some people can stick together and form small stone-like deposits called gallstones. These can be harmless, but if a stone escapes the gallbladder and enters the passageway between the gallbladder and the intestines called the bile duct, it can cause intense pain. Some people have their gallbladder removed if they experience pain regularly, and they can live normal lives without it.

Key to plate

1: **Gallbladder**
A pouch-shaped organ that stores the bile made by the liver. Bile helps to digest fats and is released into the duodenum of the small intestine after eating.

2: **Duodenum**
The first section of the small intestine is curved in shape. The openings of the common bile duct (from the gallbladder and liver) and the pancreatic duct are in the duodenum.

3: **Pancreas**
Pancreatic juice is produced in the pancreas and emptied into the duodenum.

4: **Gallbladder with gallstones**
Quite often, the salts within bile can form little deposits, like stones, that sit within the gallbladder. Normally, these gallstones are harmless, but if one escapes the gallbladder, it can block the tube running between the gallbladder and the duodenum and cause severe pain and inflammation.

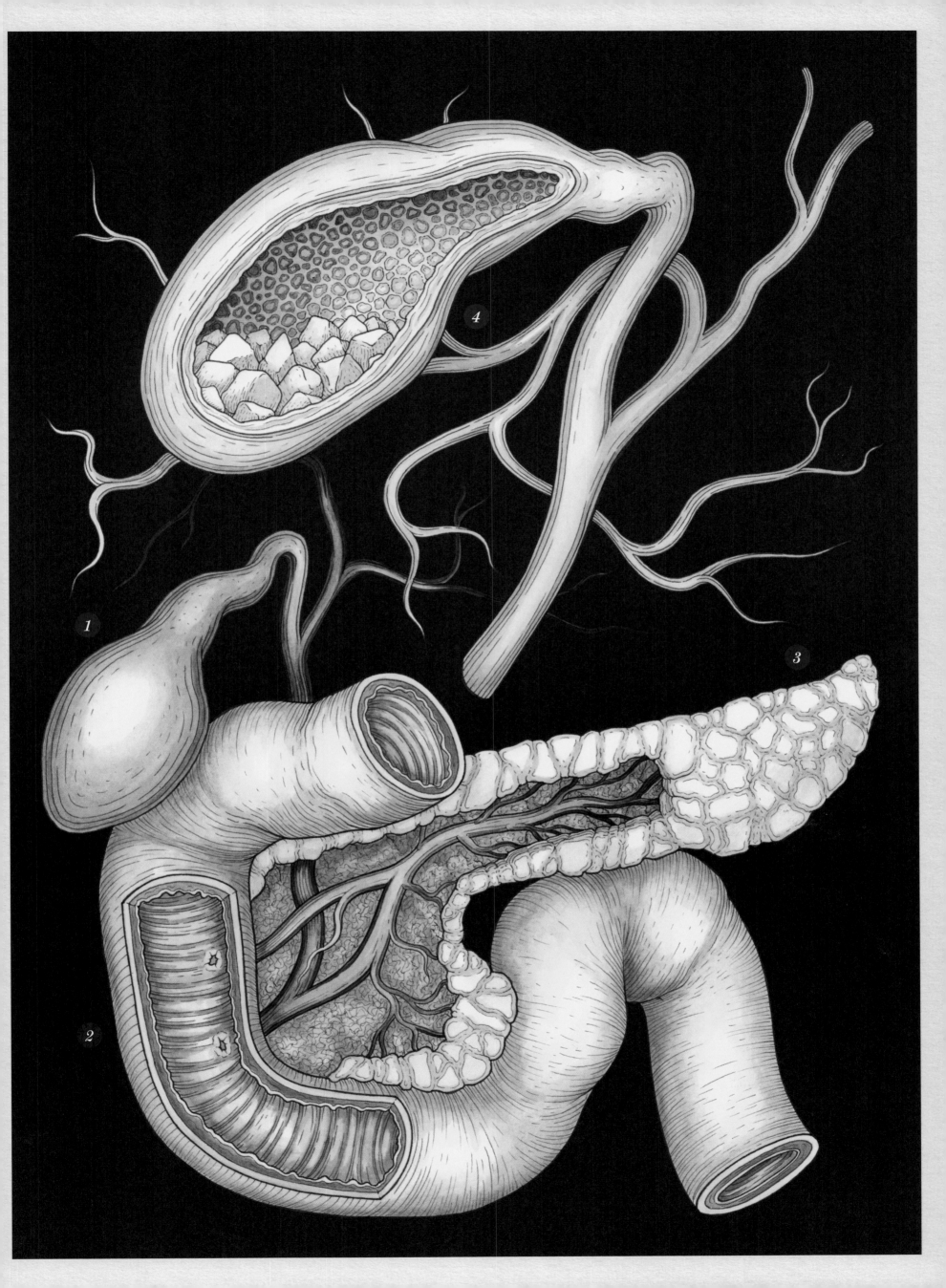

The Urinary System

The body's own plumbing system, the urinary system, is a collection of organs responsible for taking waste products from the blood and turning them into urine. The entire system sits within the abdomen and the pelvis. The two kidneys are found high up on the back wall of the abdomen, close to the liver on the right and the stomach and small intestine on the left. The kidneys do most of the hard work in the urinary system, as they are where urine is made. The rest of the system is a collection of passageways and areas for storing urine until it leaves the body.

Once urine has been made in the kidneys (see page 56), it drips down the thin tubes of the ureters, each about 1 foot/30 centimeters long. Smooth muscle in the ureters contract to push urine down to the muscular bag of the bladder, where the urine is stored. The bladder stretches as it fills with urine and can hold around 17 to 20 fluid ounces/500 to 600 milliliters at once. Special nerve sensors in the wall of the bladder get stretched as the bladder fills, letting the brain know that you need to urinate well before the bladder is full. Urine leaves the body through a thin pipe called the urethra.

Urine is mostly water but also contains waste products such as urea, which is made when proteins are broken down, and toxic chemicals the body cannot process. It also contains the chemical urobilin, which is produced when the body recycles old blood cells and is what gives urine its yellowish color. The color of urine lets us know how well hydrated a person is: a light color shows high water content, whereas a dark color means the pigment is more concentrated and that the person has not had much water. This is an easy way to see if you are becoming dehydrated—most people should drink around 1/2 gallon/2 liters of water a day.

--- *Key to plate* ---

1: **Blood supply to the kidney (renal artery)**
Oxygenated blood from the heart enters the kidneys here for filtration.

2: **Blood supply from the kidney (renal vein)**
Deoxygenated blood leaves the kidneys here.

3: **Left kidney**
Positioned high in the body, the right and left kidneys both produce urine.

4: **Right kidney**
The right kidney is usually slightly lower in the body than the left kidney. This is because the large liver takes up a lot of room on the right side.

5: **Ureters (right and left)**
The ureters are two long muscular tubes. They connect each kidney to the bladder, providing a pathway for urine to travel along.

6: **Bladder**
The bladder sits in the pelvis and stores urine until it is ready to leave the body.

7: **Urinary sphincter**
This ring of muscle controls the emptying of the bladder.

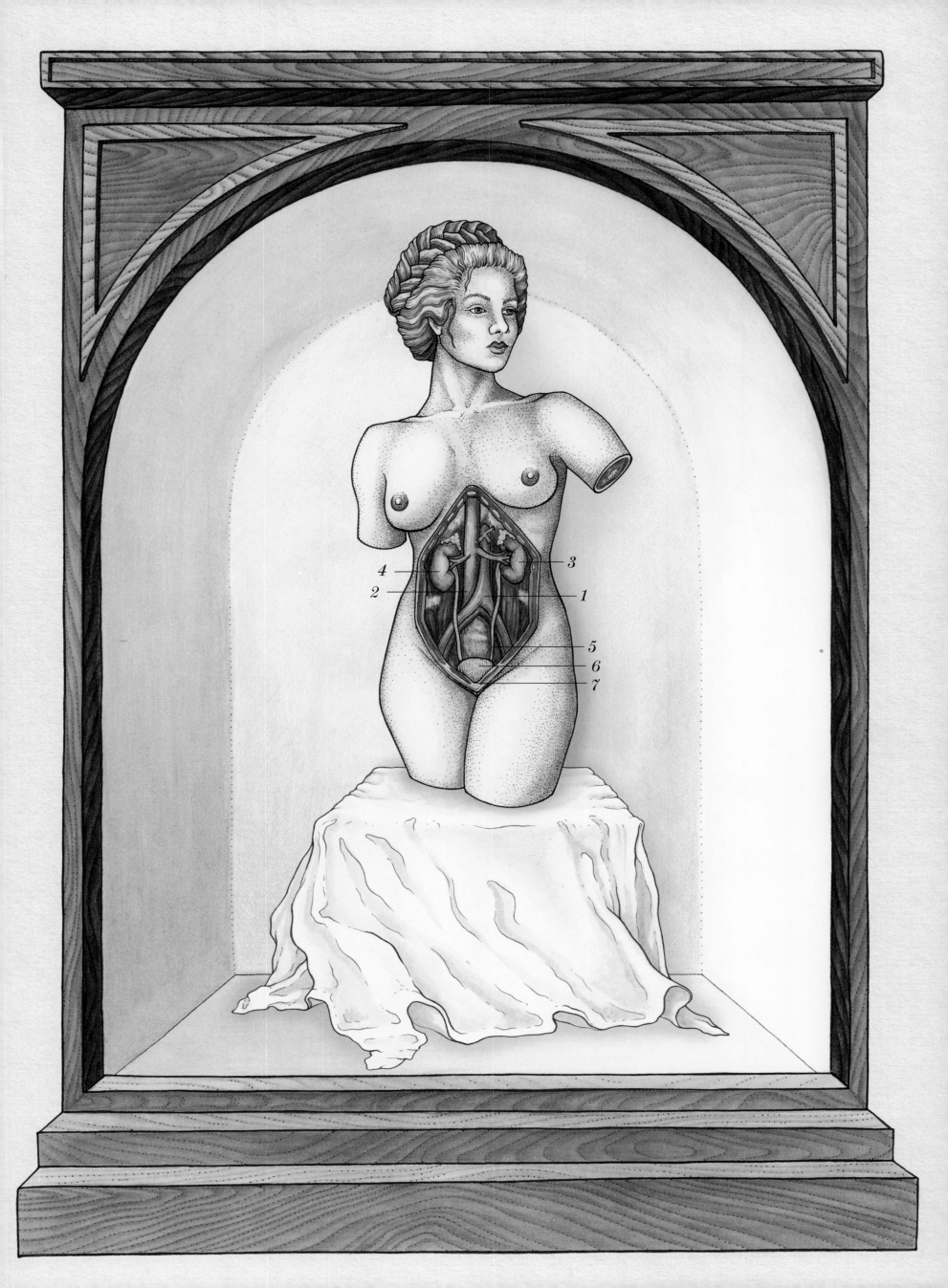

The Kidneys

The two bean-shaped kidneys are positioned toward the back of the abdomen just beneath the rib cage. Each one is about 4 to 6 inches/10 to 15 centimeters tall and works tirelessly to clean the body's blood. They do this by pumping blood through over one million tiny filters called nephrons. These remove waste products made during the body's chemical reactions, pass the toxins into our urine, and reabsorb any substances the body needs to keep. To do this, the kidneys have an extensive blood supply, receiving 20 percent of the body's blood volume at any time. It is estimated that all the blood inside the body is passed through the kidneys over forty times a day.

The kidneys also have vital roles in the overall balance of water and salts in the body. If the body is low on either, the kidneys can absorb more from the blood they are filtering, reducing the amount of urine made. On the other hand, if there is too much fluid in the blood, the kidneys can stop absorbing and the body will create more urine.

Healthy kidney function is vital to living a normal life. Thankfully, if one kidney gets damaged or stops working, the other can take over. This means it is possible to live with just one kidney. If both kidneys stop working, though, the blood cannot be cleaned and dangerous disease-causing toxins start to build up. People without a working kidney need to have dialysis, a process in which blood is pumped out of the body and through an external machine that filters their blood. This process takes several hours and has to be carried out around three times a week. A potential way to help treat kidney disease is by organ transplantation, where a working kidney is transferred into a patient from a living or recently deceased donor. Kidney transplants have been performed for over fifty years with very good success rates. Interestingly, if a patient receives a new, working kidney, it is placed in the area of the pelvis rather than the normal kidney position in the abdomen, and the nonworking kidneys are not usually removed.

Key to plate

1: **Right kidney**
The right kidney sits lower than the left because of the large liver on the right side of the abdomen.

2: **Left kidney**
a) Renal artery: A large blood vessel that supplies oxygen-rich blood to the kidneys
b) Renal vein: This blood vessel drains oxygen-poor blood from the kidneys and takes it back to the heart.
c) Renal cortex

d) Medulla: The cortex and medulla are where blood is filtered through millions of tiny units called nephrons.

3: **Ureter**
A long muscular tube that connects the kidney to the bladder

4: **Adrenal gland**
These glands are part of the endocrine system and are responsible for producing hormones such as adrenaline and noradrenaline.

5: **Nephron**
These twisted tubes are the filtration unit of the kidney where urine is made.
a) The glomerulus: Blood is filtered through a sieve-like structure called the glomerulus, then into the rest of the nephron.
b) Collecting ducts: Urine is collected in tubes that direct the fluid out of the kidney toward the ureter.

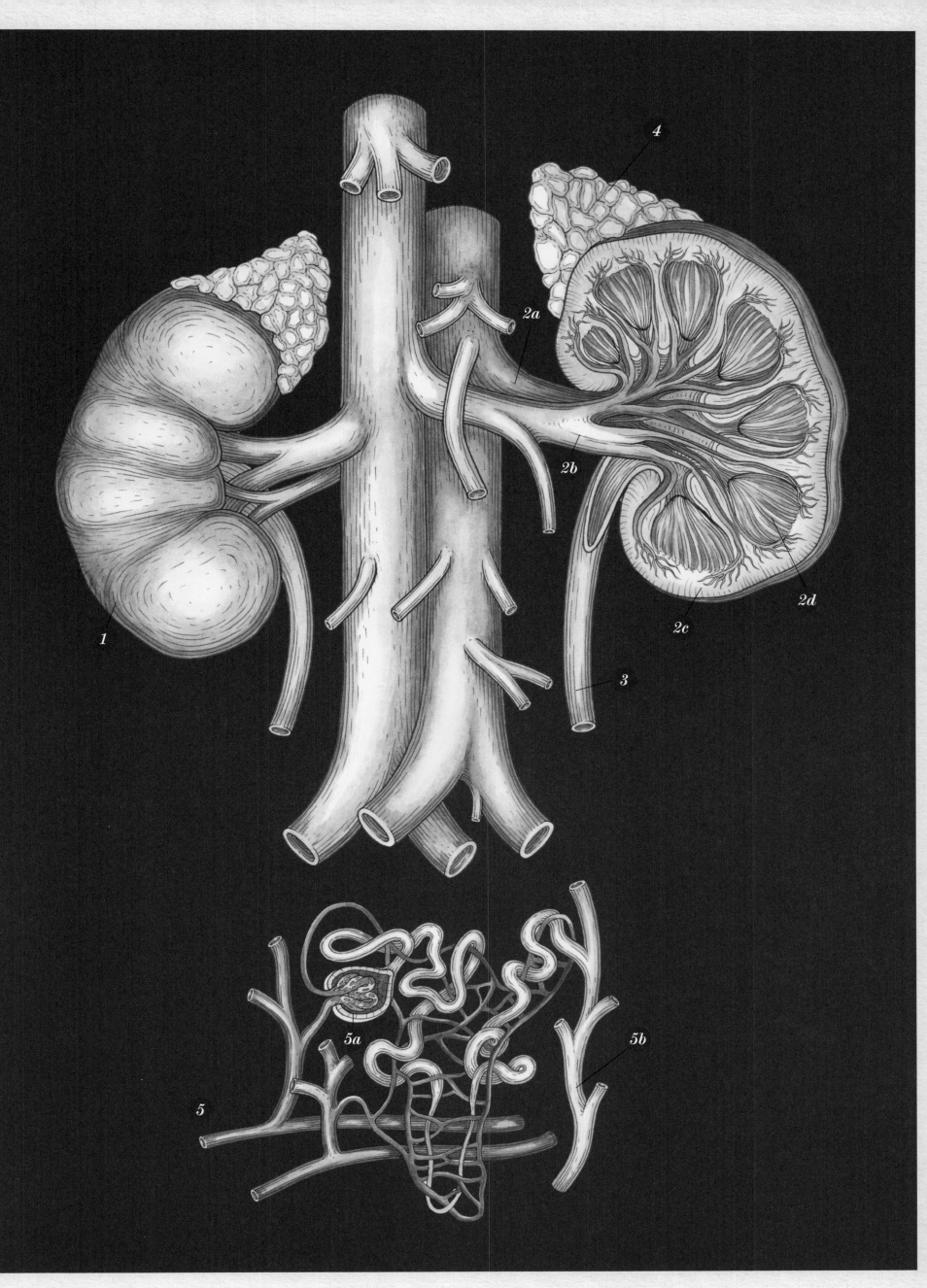

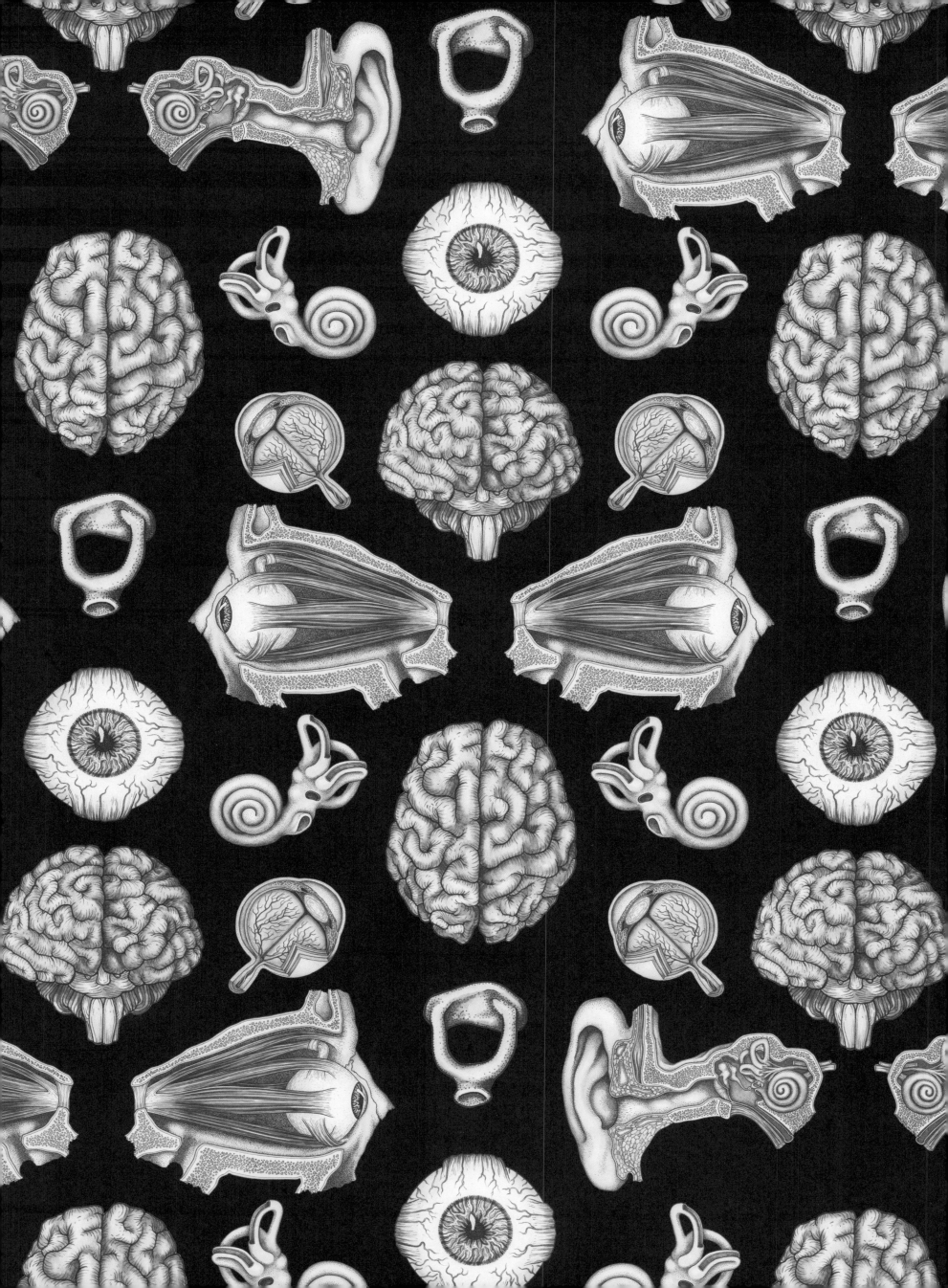

Gallery 4

The Nervous System & Special Senses

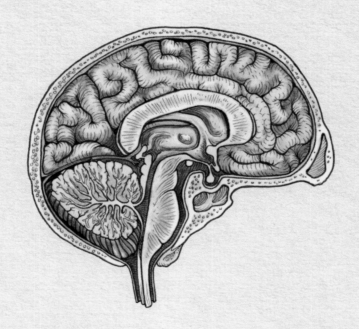

The Nervous System

The nervous system is a complex network that processes and relays information around the body like an electrical switchboard. Humans possess the most advanced nervous system we know of, and for this reason we are the only species that can talk, write, and build sophisticated machines.

The nervous system weaves through organs and tissues to connect each and every part of the body to its central control center: the brain. Sometimes described as the most elaborate supercomputer ever known, the brain processes hundreds of thousands of messages a second. These messages from the outside world and from inside your body relay to and from the brain as electrical signals. They travel along pathways called nerves, passing each other like traffic on a busy two-way street. Once the brain has taken in information, it sends a message back to the body in response. For instance, if a car appears as you are crossing the road, your eyes will see the car and send a message to the brain; the brain will process the potential danger, then send signals to make you step back onto the sidewalk. Electrical impulses travel along nerves at speeds of over 330 feet/100 meters per second, which means all that takes a fraction of a second.

The hubs of the nervous system are the brain and spinal cord. They make up the central nervous system and control most of the body's actions. These vital organs are well protected within the skull and vertebrae of the spine. The spinal cord then connects to the peripheral nervous system, which extends out into the rest of the body and is responsible for collecting sensory messages from the sense organs and delivering orders for the musculoskeletal system to move.

Key to plate

1: Central nervous system
a) Brain: This is the control center for the entire nervous system. All voluntary and many involuntary actions go through the brain.
b) Spinal cord: This long bundle of nerves connects the brain to the peripheral nervous system.

2: Peripheral nervous system
a) Spinal nerves: The spinal cord branches out to the left and right sides in thirty-one matching pairs of spinal nerves. Each pair of spinal nerves supplies a specific part of the body, and the nerve fibers travel to and from the brain.

b) Peripheral nerves: These serve the body organs and limbs, sending messages to and from the brain and spinal cord.

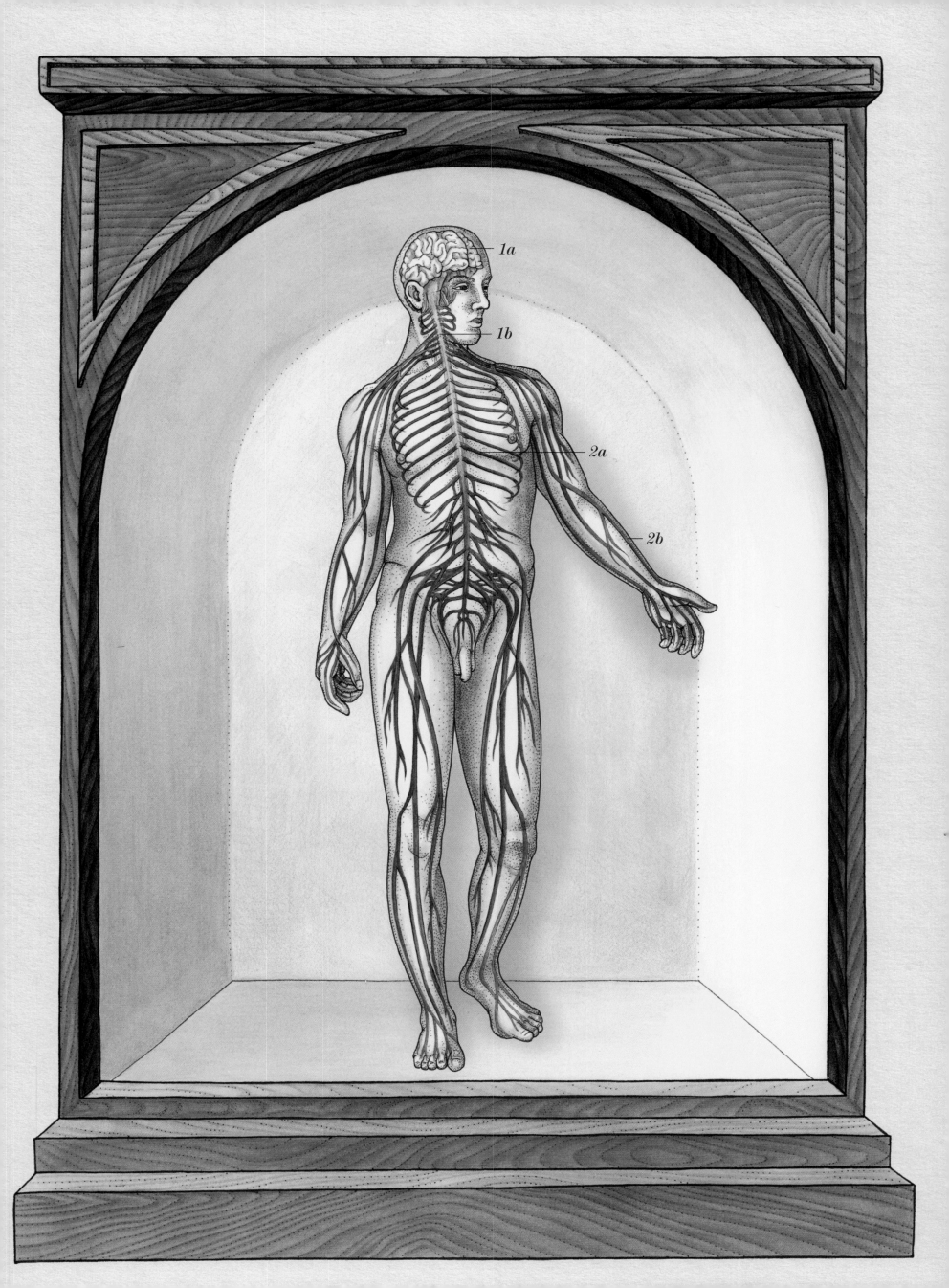

The Central Nervous System

Despite making up just 3 percent of our overall body weight, the brain uses about 20 percent of the body's energy—much more than any other organ. The brain requires all that power because it controls everything we do, from movement and breathing to thoughts, emotions, and memories.

The brain's outermost part, the cortex, has a wrinkled appearance caused by many folds of the brain tissue. If you were to spread out the cortex, its surface area would be about the size of a newspaper, but because it is folded, the brain's hundreds of billions of nerve cells can fit within the confined space of the skull. The reason our brains are so wrinkled is that they have tripled in size over the course of human evolution! The largest part of the brain is the cerebrum, which is responsible for intelligence, conscious movements, and sensations. It is split into two halves, called hemispheres, linked by a band of nerve fibers called the corpus callosum. The right side of the brain controls the left side of the body and vice versa. Within each half are areas dedicated to different functions in the body. The earliest discovery that parts of the brain control different activities was the case of Phineas Gage in 1848. An accident resulted in Phineas being injured by a metal rod right through his head. Miraculously, he survived and showed no loss of movement or sensory perception. He did, however, behave differently. Doctors concluded that the part of the brain the rod had damaged, the frontal lobe, was responsible for personality. This view is still held today, and we now know the frontal lobe is important for decision-making, planning, thinking, and emotions, which all help to shape our personalities.

Behind the cerebrum, at the very back of the brain, sits the cerebellum, a small, round structure that looks like a walnut and helps coordinate movements and balance. Hanging from the middle of the brain is the brain stem, which connects the brain to the spinal cord. The brain stem also controls the most basic activities needed to stay alive, such as breathing, digestion, and pumping the heart. It is constantly firing electrical signals rapidly from the brain to the body and back again.

Key to plate

1: Brain and spinal cord
The spinal cord extends from the center of the brain. Spinal nerves branch out down the spine, forming thirty-one pairs of nerves that travel to the left and right sides of the body. Each pair will link the brain and spinal cord to a specific body area.

2: Brain, seen from the front (anterior view)
The two cerebral hemispheres make up the main part of the brain, known as the cerebrum.

3: Brain, seen from the top (superior view)
The folds, or gyri, of the brain give a wrinkled appearance. They increase the surface area of the brain.

4: Cross section of the brain
a) Cerebrum: The largest part of the brain is responsible for higher-order functions such as thinking, learning, decision-making, and memory. It is also involved in sensory perception and the control of voluntary movements.
b) Cerebellum: This helps to coordinate movements and balance.
c) Brain stem: This controls activities like breathing, the pumping of the heart, and digestion.
d) Spinal cord

5: Lobes of the brain
These are named after the skull bones positioned above the different parts of the brain.
a) Frontal lobe
b) Parietal lobe
c) Occipital lobe
d) Temporal lobe

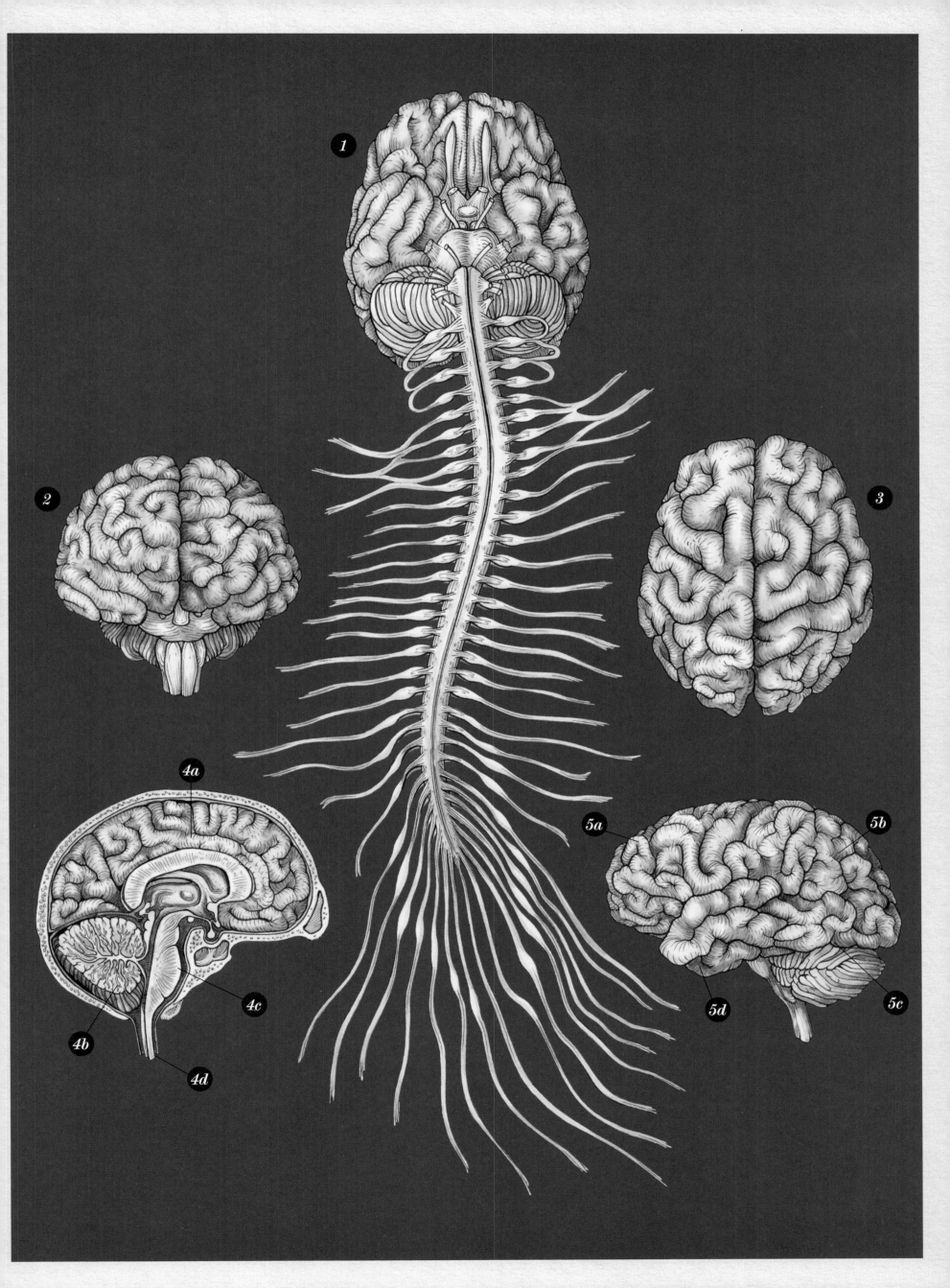

The Peripheral Nervous System

Individual nerves are made from bundles of thin nerve cells, called neurons, which run through the body like electrical wires. Most neurons have one main fiber called an axon, which sends outgoing electrical signals. Several smaller fibers called dendrites then collect incoming signals from other neurons. In between individual neurons there are small gaps called synapses. Electrical signals cannot jump across these gaps, so axons release neurotransmitters that activate the dendrites. The dendrites can then receive a signal and pass it on via their own axon. In this way, signals can be sent at incredible speeds from neuron to neuron.

The longest part of the neuron is the axon itself. Axons vary in size from less than 1 millimeter long to more than 3 feet/1 meter. Just like electrical wires need a plastic coating to retain their current, axons also have an insulating layer. This takes the form of a fatty tube, called the myelin sheath, which wraps right around the axon. Any damage to this myelin sheath reduces the ability of nerve impulses to transmit between the brain and the body, as seen in diseases such as multiple sclerosis.

The entire human body contains around 95 to 100 billion neurons. Around 80 percent of these are in the brain and spinal cord (see page 62), but the remainder are found within the peripheral nervous system (PNS). This network of nerves begins where the spinal cord branches out into thirty-one pairs of spinal nerves, traveling to the left and right sides of the body. It plays a crucial role in communication between the central nervous system and the body's senses and muscles.

The neurons of the PNS are either sensory or motor. Sensory neurons send information from sense organs, such as the eyes and ears, to the brain and spinal cord, while motor neurons send messages from the brain and spinal cord to the muscles and glands. The PNS is further divided into somatic (voluntary) neurons, which move the skeleton, and autonomic (involuntary) neurons, which control bodily functions such as breathing without us ever having to think about them.

Key to plate

1: Reflex arc

If your hand comes near a candle, pain sensors in the hand will send a message to the spinal cord. The spinal cord will process the danger without sending signals to the brain and will send motor signals telling the hand to move away from the flame. Reflex reactions enable the body to react at the first sign of danger.

2: Anatomy of a spinal nerve

a) Axon: The part of a nerve along which electrical signals are sent
b) Myelin sheath: This fatty layer acts as an insulating coating for the axon.
c) Fascicle: This is the name for a bundle of axons.
d) Perineurium: This is a coating around fascicles.
e) Blood vessels

3: Close-up of a neuron (nerve cell)

a) Cell body
b) Dendrite
c) Axon
d) Myelin sheath
e) Nerve ending

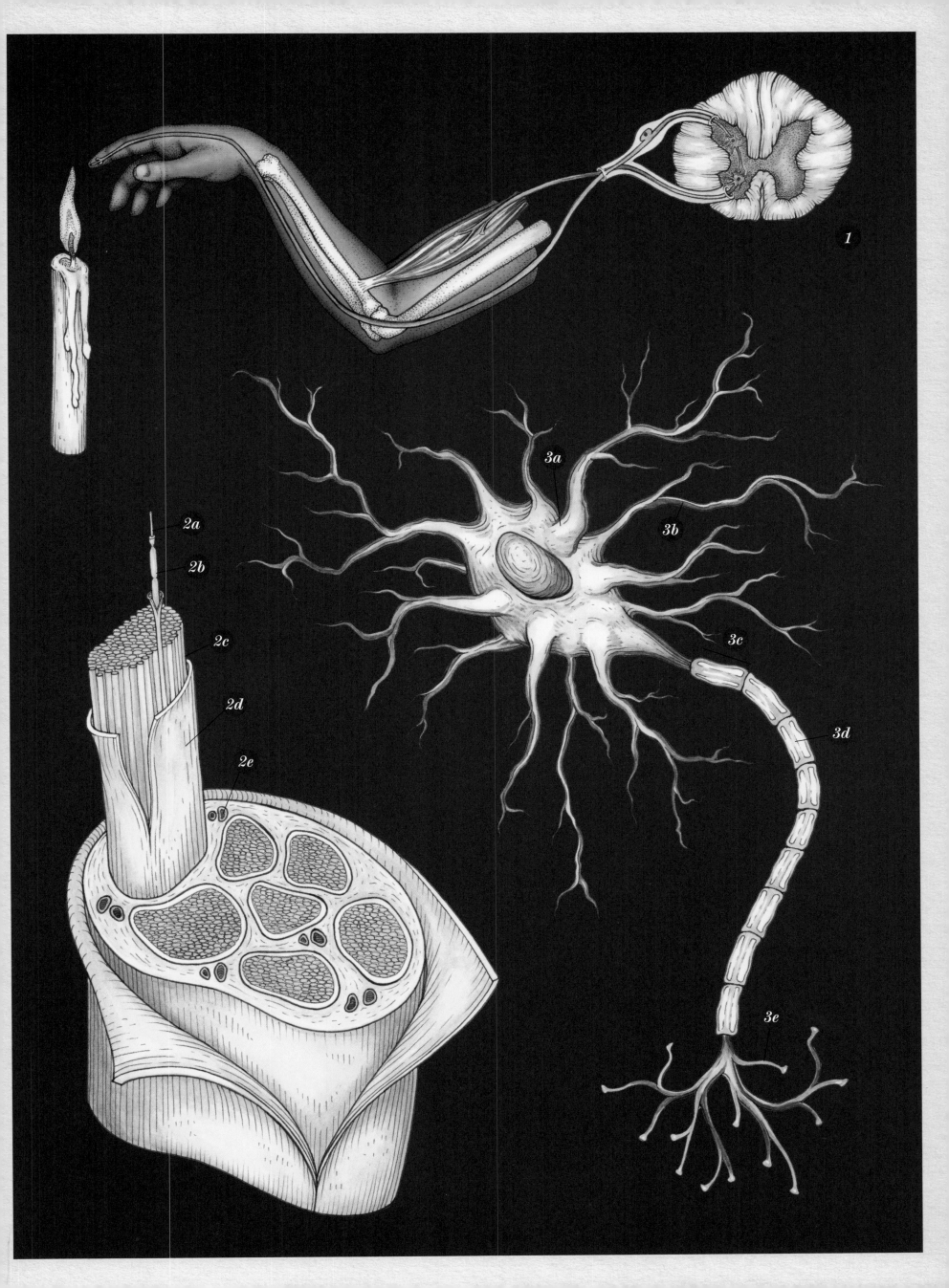

1

2a

2b

2c

2d

2e

3a

3b

3c

3d

3e

The Eyes

The eyes are a pair of ball-shaped organs set within the skull in two spherical holes called orbits. Each eyeball is about the size of a ping-pong ball, and its job is to receive light and turn this information into electrical signals that the brain can understand as images.

Light enters the eye through a small hole called the pupil, the black "dot" visible in the center of the eye. This hole is not open to the outside world; a clear shield called the cornea covers the surface of the eyeball, simultaneously protecting the eye and focusing incoming light. Because the cornea has to remain transparent, like a clean glass window, it is the only tissue in the body that does not contain a blood supply. Instead, a thin film of tears keeps the eyes wet and nourished.

Surrounding the pupil is the iris, a ring of pigmented (colored) muscle that gives eyes their color and adjusts the size of the pupil. When exposed to bright light, the muscles of the iris move automatically, making the pupil much smaller and reducing the amount of light that can pass through. The opposite happens in low light, and the pupil expands to let more light in. After light has entered the eye, it is passed through the lens, a small clear structure that bends the light and focuses it onto the back of the eyeball. Tiny muscles on either side of the lens adjust its shape, making it fatter to view objects close by and thinner if objects are farther away. If these muscles lose their strength, glasses can help the eye focus the light and stop objects from appearing blurry.

The back of the eye, known as the retina, is lined with millions of light-detecting sensory cells. These translate light messages into electrical signals for the brain to receive. About seven million of these cells are a type called cones, which detect colors but are unable to function well in low light. The other 100 million cells are called rods. These are much more sensitive to light, so they work well in low light, though they do not detect color. This is why scenes appear to be black-and-white at nighttime. Once the rods and cones have received information, it is transmitted to the brain via the optic nerve at the back of each eye. Incredibly, this whole process happens in a fraction of a second, and it is thought that the human eye can process nearly one thousand frames, or images, per second.

Key to plate

1: **The retina (back of the eye)**
Blood vessels cover the back of the eye around the fovea: a small pit where the cones are tightly packed, and where light rays are focused. The back of the eye also contains the optic nerve, linking the eye to the brain.

2: **The eye muscles**
a) Front view
b) Side view
Three pairs of skeletal muscles attach to the outside of each eye, enabling them to move. Their movements are voluntary, but the coordination of left and right eye movements together is involuntary.

3: **Iris and pupil**
The iris is a ring of pigmented tissue that surrounds the pupil. The pupil is a hole in the center of the iris. This is where light enters the eye to travel toward the retina.

4: **Inside the eyeball**
a) Cornea: This is the clear outer covering of the eyeball.
b) Iris: The pigmented muscle
c) Pupil: Where light enters the eye
d) Lens: Where light is focused. The shape of the lens can be changed by muscles on either side of it.
e) Vitreous humor. A clear, gel-like substance filling the eyeball
f) Retina: This is the sensory layer at the back of the eyeball
g) Optic nerve: This carries sensory information from the eye to the brain.

5: **Tear production (interior structure)**
a) Tear (lacrimal) gland
b) Tear duct
Eyelashes, eyelids, and tear production all protect the eyes from damage. Tears keep the surface of the eyeball wet and can be used to wash out the eye. This is why eyes begin to "water" when they become irritated. Excess tears spill out of the eye or drain into the nose via the tear duct, which is why a runny nose is normal when crying.

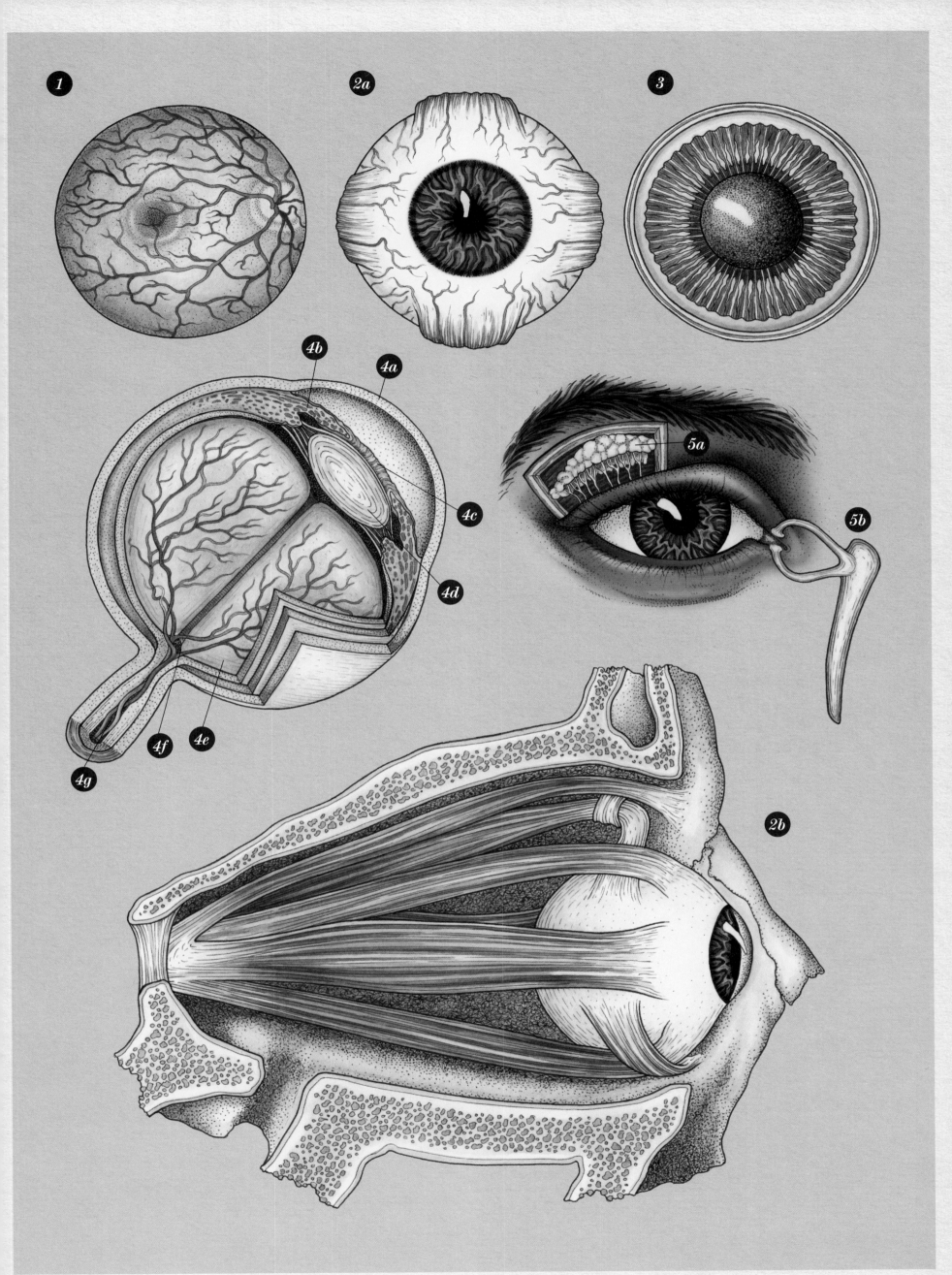

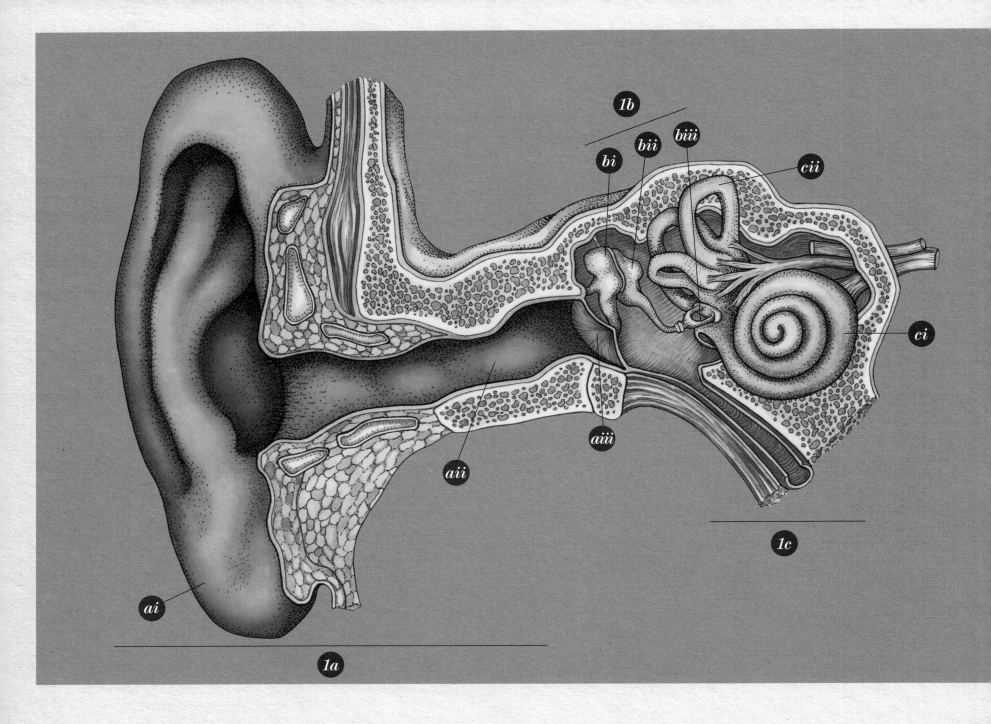

The Ears

The part of the ear we can see is in fact just the outer section of an intricate organ that extends deep within our head. Each of the three regions—the outer ear, the middle ear, and the inner ear—has a distinct function. The outer ear's role is to funnel sounds, the middle ear converts sounds to vibrations, and the inner ear converts vibrations to nerve signals the brain can process. Made from a material called elastic cartilage, the outer ear collects sounds from all around us and directs them into the ear canal. This passageway runs 1 inch/2.5 centimeters from the opening on the surface of the skull to the eardrum, a tight membrane that vibrates when sound waves reach it. The eardrum also acts as a physical barrier to stop objects from entering the deeper parts of the ear.

On the other side of the eardrum lies the middle ear, an air-filled space containing three tiny but extremely important bones: the ossicles. These bones, called the hammer, anvil, and stirrup, connect the eardrum to part of the inner ear called the cochlea. Named for its resemblance to a snail's shell (*cochlea* is derived from the Greek word for "snail"), the cochlea is a tightly coiled tube about the size of a pea, filled with fluid and thousands of tiny hairs. When sound waves make the eardrum vibrate, the movement passes through the ossicles to the cochlea. The fluid and hairs in the cochlea move, creating electrical impulses that are sent to the brain and decoded as sounds. Sometimes, the tiny hairs in the cochlea can get damaged by very loud noises or can deteriorate over

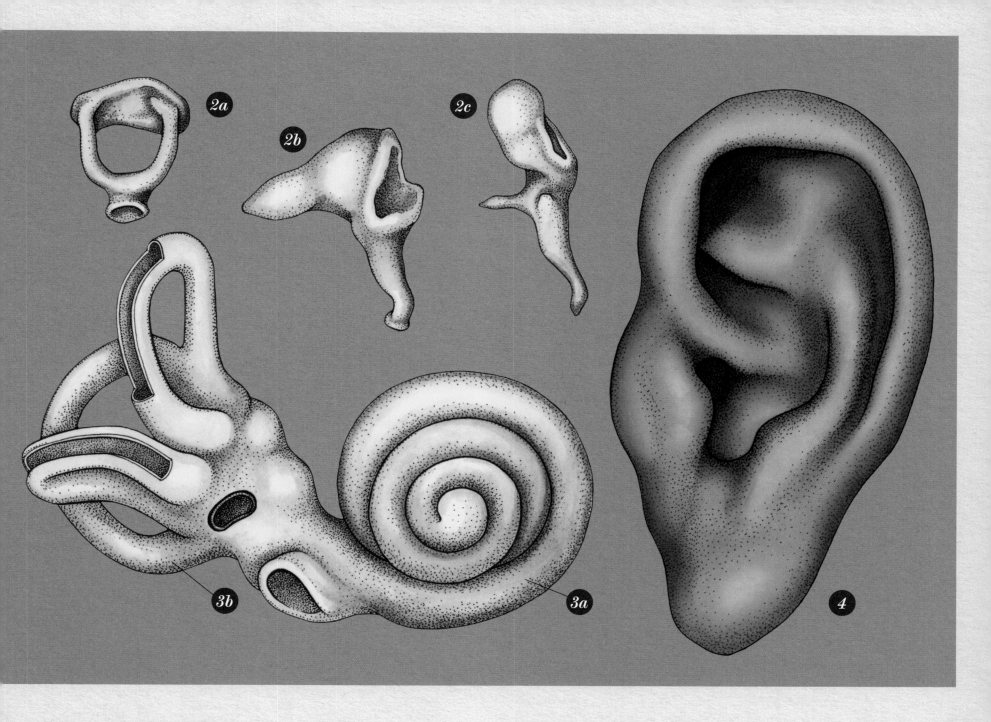

time. This is why it is common for elderly people to have problems with their hearing.

Aside from their role in hearing, the ears are also central to our sense of balance. Within the inner ear is a series of thin, rounded tubes called the semicircular canals. These sit next to the cochlea and are also filled with fluid and more tiny hairs. The fluid and hairs in the semicircular canals move with every change in position of the head, letting the brain know which way up we are. The brain can then respond to changes in position quickly and stop us from falling over. This doesn't always work as well as we would hope, though, and dizziness occurs when the fluid in the semicircular canals keeps moving even though we are standing still.

─────────────── *Key to plate* ───────────────

1: **Ear**
a) Outer ear: This consists of the pinna *(i)*, which leads into the ear canal *(ii)*. At the end of the ear canal lies the eardrum *(iii)*.
b) Middle ear: The three smallest bones in the body, the hammer *(i)*, anvil *(ii)*, and stirrup *(iii)*, transmit the vibrations of the eardrum toward the inner ear.
c) Inner ear: The cochlea *(i)* and semicircular canals *(ii)* convert

the vibrations of sound waves into electrical signals for the brain to interpret.

2: **Ossicles**
a) Stapes (stirrup)
b) Incus (anvil)
c) Malleus (hammer)

3: **Inner ear**
a) Cochlea
b) Semicircular canals

4: **Pinna (outer ear)**
The outer ear acts solely as a funnel for sounds entering the middle ear. However, it also has some interesting characteristics. The shape of an individual's outer ear is unique to that person, and it has been suggested that the pattern of the ears could be as distinctive as a fingerprint! Also, the outer ear is one of the few parts of the body to continue growing in adulthood, particularly in males.

The Nose & Tongue

Our senses of smell and taste can detect and recognize a staggering number of substances. These senses can also alert us to a potential danger—for example, toxic chemicals or rotten food—but they are not usually considered essential for modern humans. Yet many years ago, our senses were far more important for our survival. The repulsion created by disgusting smells or tastes helped to keep the body safe from life-threatening infections that could be found in feces, dirty water, or bacteria-ridden food, which would once have been daily encounters.

It is thought that the average human can detect several billion different odors. Human sense of smell is most sensitive at birth to help newborns recognize their mother. Smell works by detecting odor molecules that float in the air around us. When we breathe, they enter the nostrils and pass into the nasal cavity—a large space behind the external nose. The roof of the nasal cavity contains millions of receptor cells that detect odors and transfer the smell into an electrical impulse. This signal travels to the brain via a connection called the olfactory nerve.

Although our sense of smell is said to be ten thousand times more powerful than our sense of taste, the two are closely linked, and food tastes different if the ability to smell is impaired. This is something you might have encountered before, especially if you've eaten while you have a bad cold or pinched your nose while chewing food.

Thousands of taste sensors are found on the top surface of the tongue, on little bumps called papillae. More commonly known as taste buds, these special sensors detect chemicals in the food we eat and send messages to the brain. They can detect five basic flavors: sweet, sour, salty, bitter, and umami, meaning "savory" in the Japanese language.

--- *Key to plate* ---

1: Nose
a) External nose: Mostly made of cartilage, the external nose is where odor molecules enter the nasal cavity through the nostrils (*i*).
b) Nasal cavity: This space inside the skull is home to the olfactory nerves

(*i*), which detect odor molecules and transmit the sensory impulse toward the brain.

2: Tongue
The tongue sits in the oral cavity and is made up of several muscles.

Many thousands of taste buds (or papillae) cover the top surface and are responsible for detecting one of the five different categories of taste sensation: sweet, sour, salty, bitter, and umami.

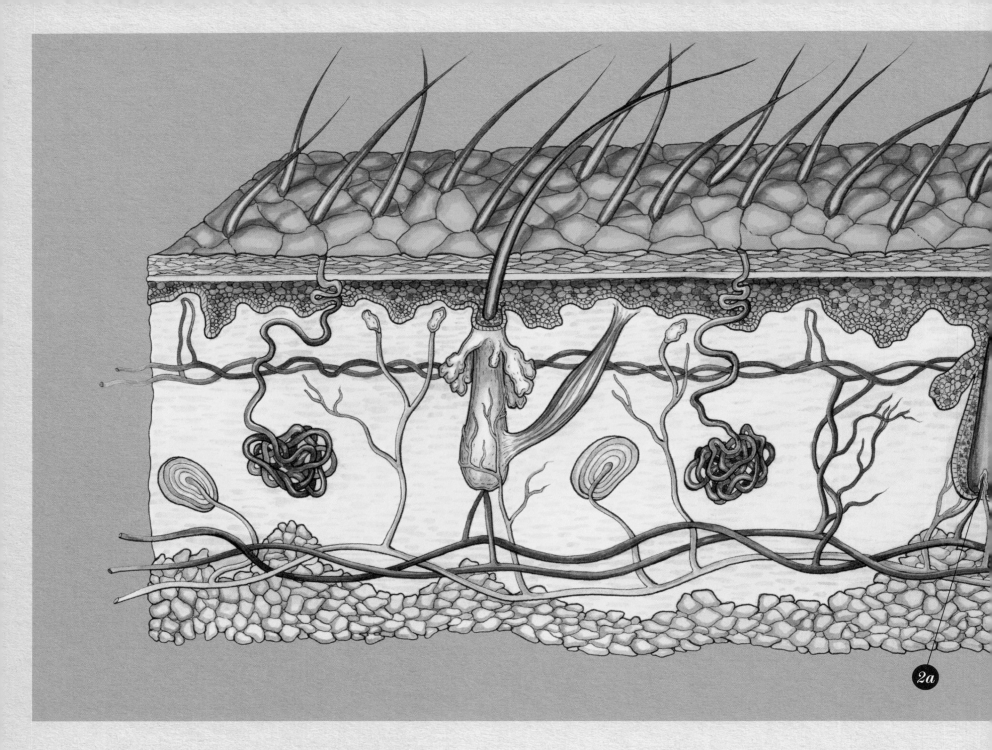

2a

The Skin

Forming our whole outer body covering, the skin is part of the integumentary system, a collection of structures that includes skin, hair, and nails and forms a flexible barrier between us and the outside world. Tiny touch sensors lie deep within the skin. Apart from being the most visible body organ, the skin is the largest organ by both weight and surface area. Surprisingly, it was often ignored by the early anatomists and usually discarded to access the organs and tissues beneath. As scientific discoveries progressed and instruments like the microscope were invented, anatomists were able to explore the skin in greater detail and determine the many important jobs it has.

Skin is made up of two layers. The top layer, the epidermis, is made from several sheets of skin cells that create a protective, waterproof wrapping around the body. Skin cells in the epidermis are always hard at work, growing, multiplying, and moving nearer to the surface of the skin as if they are on a conveyor belt. In fact, the very top cells are actually dead, and millions of skin cells fall off each day. Other cells in the epidermis produce melanin, a protective substance that shields the skin from harmful sun rays. When the body is exposed to direct sunlight, the skin may produce extra melanin in defense, which causes the skin to darken or tan. Underneath the epidermis lies the dermis, a thicker layer made from strong and stretchy proteins. It contains hairs

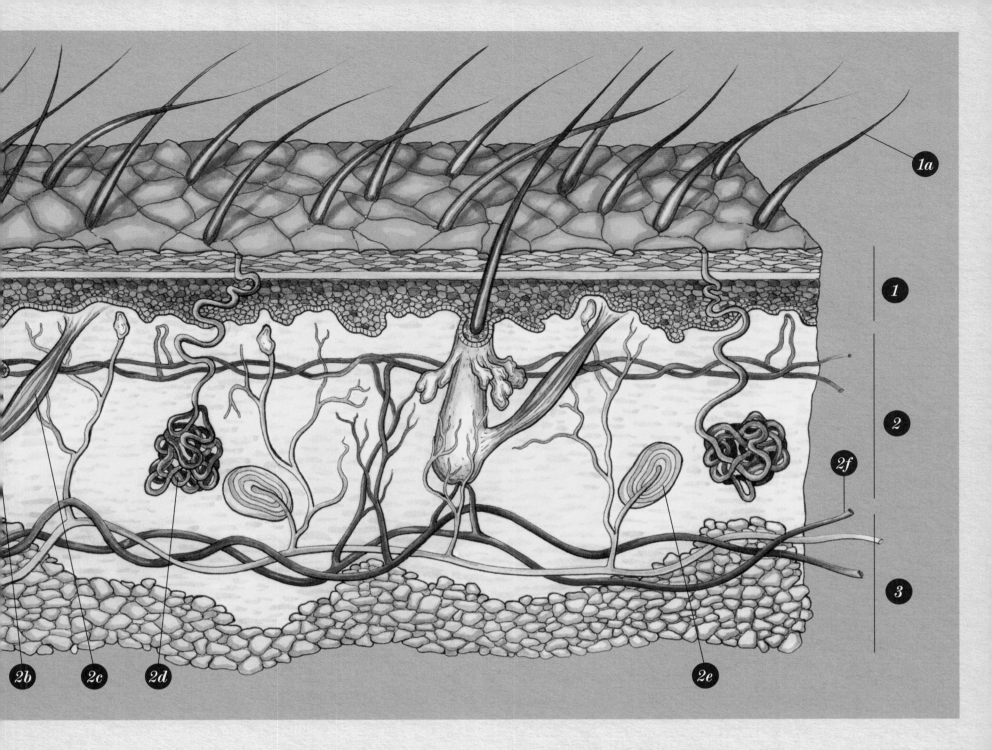

and sweat glands and is home to millions of nerve endings—the sensory receptors that give us our sense of touch. They are found all over the body but are more concentrated in regions such as the face and the fingertips.

Sensory receptors respond to different types of stimuli depending on their type. Mechanoreceptors respond to a mechanical stimulus, such as pressure or vibrations. Sensors that respond to hot or cold temperatures are called thermoreceptors, and those that react to pain are called nociceptors. The final type of sensor are the proprioceptors, which help tell us what position our body is in and therefore help us to coordinate our movements. A sense of touch is crucial for keeping us safe; without it we would not be able to feel our feet on the ground as we walk, to hold and control objects, or to feel pain. Pain in particular is crucial to protecting us from harm, as it alerts the body to danger.

Key to plate

1: Epidermis
The top layer of skin, made from multiple sheets of skin cells
a) Hair shaft

2: Dermis
a) Hair root
b) Sebaceous gland
c) Arrector pili muscle: This pulls hairs upward in goose bumps.
d) Sweat gland

e) Sensory receptor
f) Dermal blood vessels

3: Hypodermis
The underlying fat layer

73

Gallery 5

The Immune & Lymphatic Systems

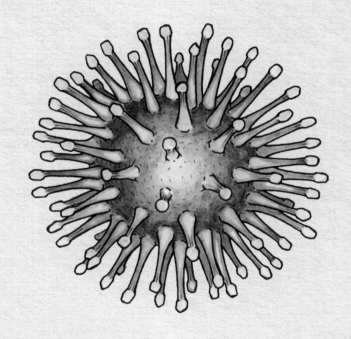

The Immune & Lymphatic Systems
Disease & Defense

The Immune
& Lymphatic
Systems

Imagine an army ready to defend your body from the millions of dangerous germs you encounter every day. This is the immune system, the body's main means of protection. Together with the lymphatic system, it is locked in a constant battle against disease.

The immune system is a collection of organs, tissues, and cells that work to defend the body from harmful bacteria or substances that do not belong. An important cell of the immune system is the white blood cell, also known as a leukocyte. Leukocytes are found in the blood (see page 32) and in areas of disease-fighting tissue, called lymphoid (or immune) organs. These include the thymus, the spleen, the tonsils, and the lymph nodes. The largest organ in the immune system is the spleen. It filters the blood, removing old or damaged blood cells from circulation. It also makes leukocytes, which produce antibodies (see page 78) to attack bacteria and viruses, and stores blood—holding around a cupful at any one time.

The lymphatic system is made of an extensive network of small vessels that run throughout the body, and lymph nodes, which are clumps of immune tissue found in the neck, armpits, and groin. Lymph nodes act like tiny sieves to filter out foreign materials in the body, swelling up if they have trapped invaders and are fighting an infection. As part of the immune system, the lymphatic system helps to tackle disease, but it also mops up excess fluid within the body.

Lymph is a watery substance that comes from liquid squeezed out of the body's cells. A buildup of this fluid would cause parts of the body to swell, so the lymphatic system sucks any excess through tiny, thin-walled lymphatic vessels surrounding blood capillaries. The lymph travels around the body through a network of lymphatic vessels, being cleaned along the way before eventually being emptied into the large veins near the heart. Here the lymph mixes with the blood before being pumped around the body.

Key to plate

1: The tonsils
Three sets of tonsils (lymphoid tissue) in the neck region help to fight infection. These can become swollen when someone has tonsillitis.

2: Lymph nodes in armpit
Lymph nodes are small collections of lymphoid tissue in the armpit, neck, and groin region. They often swell up if a person is fighting an infection.

3: The thymus gland
The thymus is a gland that sits in between the breastbone and the lungs. It is where special defense cells called T lymphocytes (see page 78) mature. The thymus is most active until teenage years, when it begins to shrink and be replaced by fat.

4: The thoracic duct
This is the largest of the lymphatic

vessels in the body. It transports lymph from the rest of the body to the veins near the heart, where the lymph returns to the circulating blood.

5: The spleen
A soft, dark-red organ shaped like a jellyfish. The spleen stores blood, filters it, and makes white blood cells.

Disease & Defense

Microbes, or microorganisms, are tiny living things too small to be seen with the naked eye. They include bacteria, viruses, microscopic animals, and fungi, and they can be found all around us. The human body is full of microbes, too, many of which are helpful to processes such as digestion. For example, lactobacteria help to digest the sugars in milk, and bifidobacteria help the gut work properly. However, some types of microbes are dangerous to the body and can make us sick. It is the job of the white blood cells, or leukocytes, to find these bacteria and remove them.

There are several types of leukocytes, each with different jobs to do. Macrophages are very large cells that destroy foreign objects by capturing them. Their name means "big eater" in ancient Greek. One of these is the lymphocyte, of which there are two types: T lymphocytes and B lymphocytes. T lymphocytes look for germs that could cause illness, or for abnormal cells with the potential to form disease such as cancer. B lymphocytes produce proteins called antibodies, which stick to a harmful germ like flags to show other white blood cells that the invader needs to be destroyed. The more antibodies produced, the greater the response to the invader will be. Once antibodies have been produced, the immune system will remember how to fight that invader in the future. This is known as immunity. The body also builds up immunity through vaccinations, which are injections that introduce the body to an inactive form of a microbe. Many serious diseases such as polio and smallpox have been eradicated because of the introduction of vaccinations.

Compared to red blood cells, which have a lifespan of about 120 days, white blood cells only last around three days, so they are constantly produced in the bone marrow (see page 10) and released into the blood and lymphatic tissues. The number of leukocytes in the body, called the white cell count, is a good indicator of disease. A low white cell count means a person is susceptible to disease, because the number of cells available to fight harmful substances is reduced. A high white cell count often means that the patient has an infection, because white blood cells are multiplying in order to seek out and destroy an invader.

Key to plate

1: **Bacteria**
a) Bacilli: These rod-shaped bacteria, such as *E.coli* (*i*), live in the digestive tract and can be single or joined together in long chains.
b) Cocci: Ball- or sphere-shaped, these bacteria exist on their own or joined with other cocci to make diplococcus (*i*) or staphylococcus (*ii*) bacteria.
c) Spiralis: Twisted or curved in shape

2: **Viruses**
a) Helical: Shaped like a tube, these viruses have a thick outer coating.
b) Polyhedral: These viruses are shaped like a dodecahedron, with twelve sides. A subset of this virus type are the spherical viruses (*i*).
c) Complex: These have a spiraling, helix-shaped tail and a head with a polyhedral shape. These viruses are called bacteriophages, a class of virus known to only infect bacteria.

3: **Leukocytes (white blood cells)**
a) Neutrophils: The commonest type of leukocytes, neutrophils make up about 60 percent of them. They destroy bacteria and damaged tissue.
b) Lymphocytes: These make up 20–40 percent of all leukocytes. B lymphocytes make proteins called antibodies that help identify cells to be destroyed; T lymphocytes attack foreign material in the body, such as viruses or cancerous cells.
c) Monocytes: The largest of all the leukocytes, monocyte cells turn into macrophages that destroy dead cells and bacteria by swallowing them.
d) Eosinophils: These cells help control allergic reactions and destroy parasitic worms.
e) Basophils: The rarest type of leukocyte, these are important in fighting parasitic infections and in regulating allergic responses, such as our responses to pollen or insect stings.

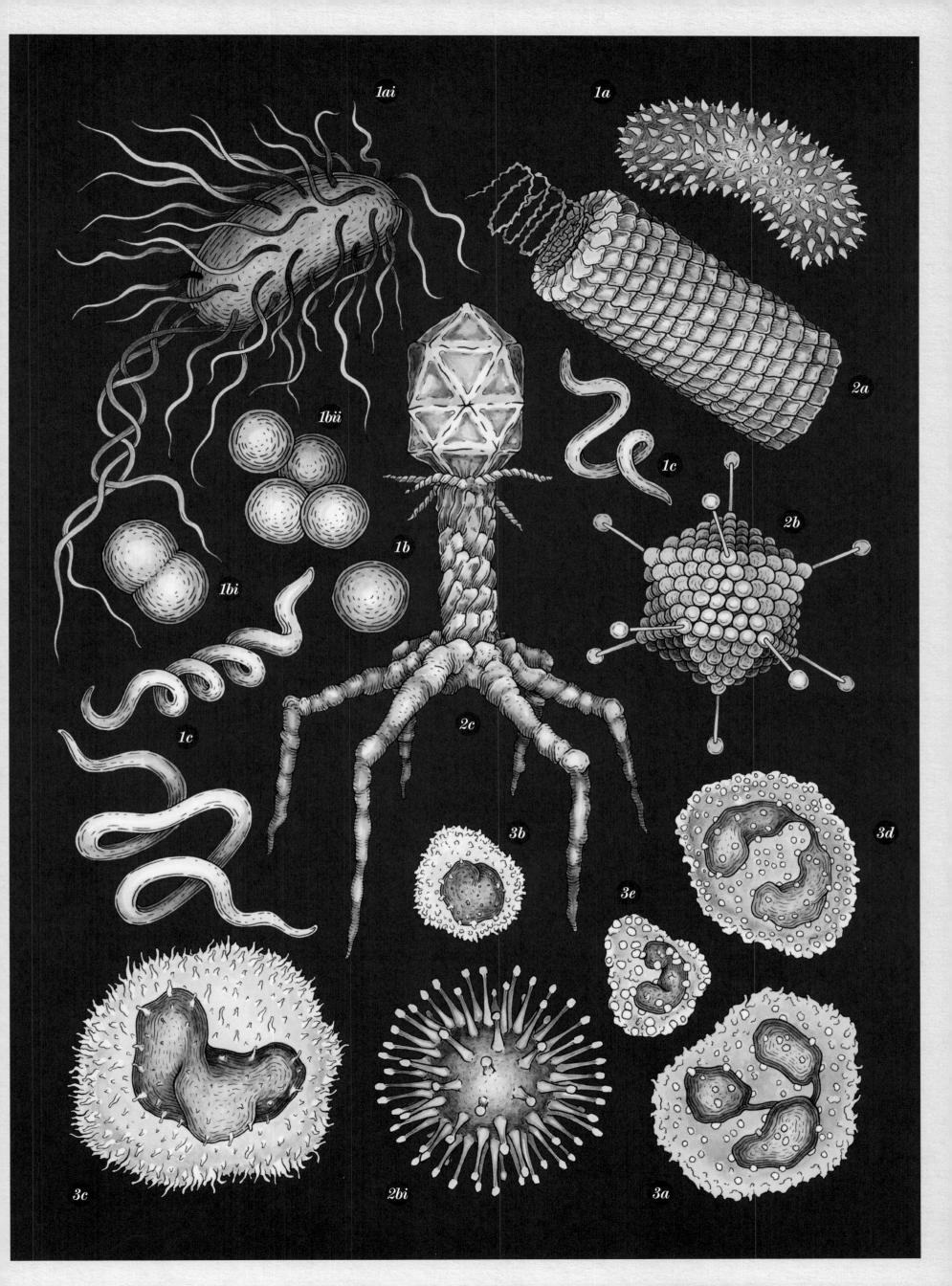

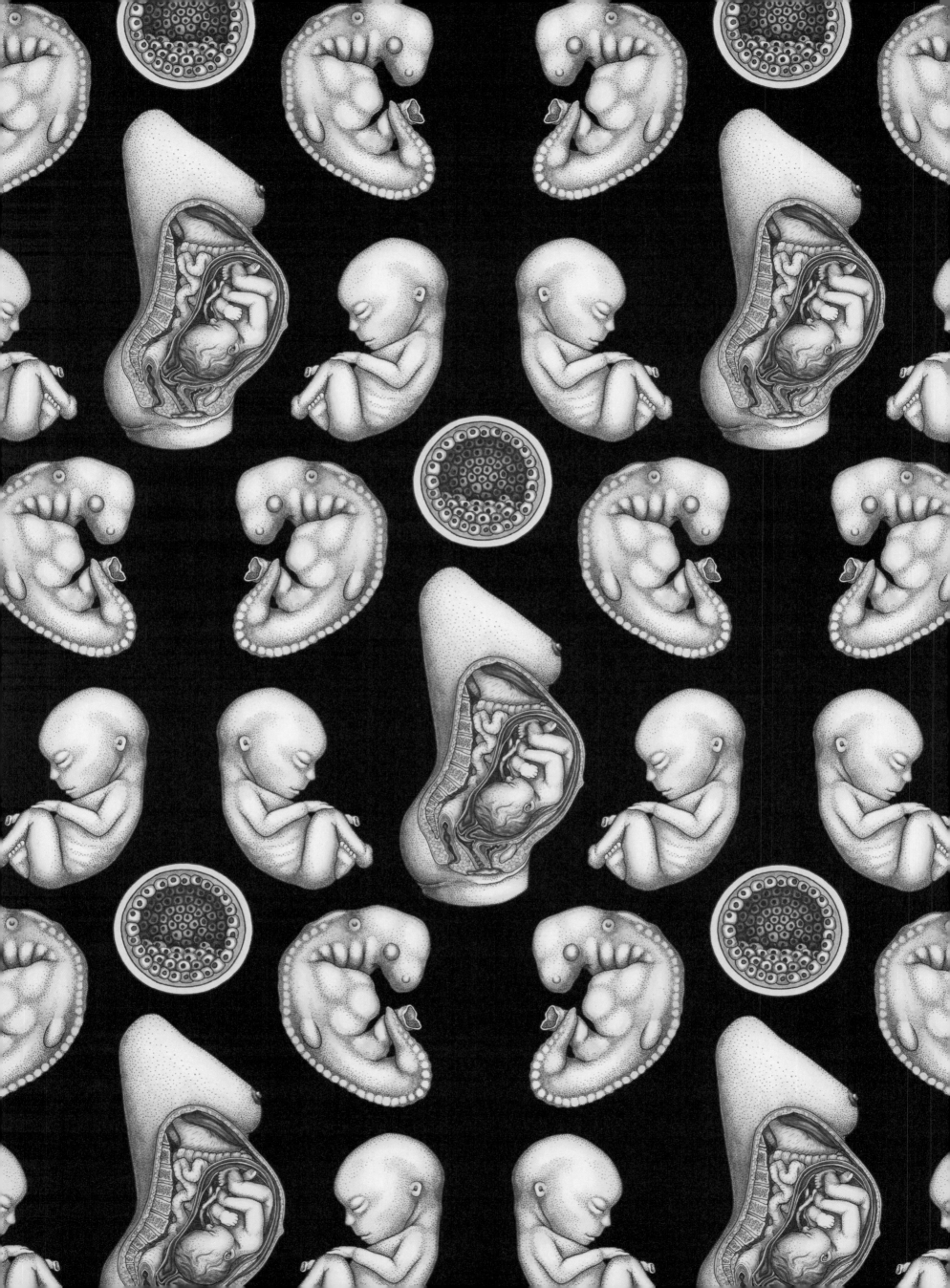

Gallery 6

The Endocrine & Reproductive Systems

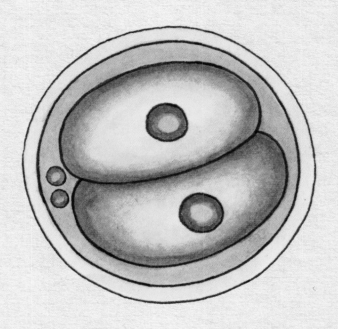

The Endocrine System

Over sixty different chemical messengers circulate in the blood, delivering instructions to various parts of the body. These messengers are called hormones. They control our growth, our sleep, and even our moods. The amount of hormones in our blood can vary depending on age, sex, and even time of day! Crucially, hormones enable our body parts to "talk" to one another—just like the nervous system uses electrical impulses to send messages around the body. The difference is that hormones travel in the blood, so their messages take much longer to be delivered than nervous signals—a bit like the difference in speed between mailing a letter and sending an email.

Hormones are produced by specialized cells in the glands and organs of the endocrine system. One of the main endocrine organs is the pancreas, which makes the hormone insulin to control blood sugar levels. If the pancreas is unable to make insulin, the disease diabetes develops and patients need to receive injections of insulin to keep their blood sugar levels under control.

If you have ever been frightened or excited, you will be familiar with the powerful hormone adrenaline. Produced by the adrenal glands above the kidneys, this hormone makes your heart beat faster, your breathing rate increase, and your pupils enlarge. You may become pale as blood is diverted away from the skin toward the muscles in your limbs, and your body may tense all over. These reactions happen automatically when adrenaline prepares your body to escape or confront danger in what is called the fight-or-flight response. Although usually activated by a physical threat, this intense reaction can have emotional triggers, too.

Key to plate

1: **Hypothalamus**
This part of the brain sends messages to the pituitary gland, instructing it to produce hormones that affect how you feel and control hunger, thirst, and body temperature.

2: **Pituitary gland**
This gland secretes hormones that control growth and development, including the sex hormones that trigger puberty and the maintenance and development of sex cells.

3: **Pineal gland**
This gland in the brain produces hormones that regulate sleep.

4: **Thyroid gland**
Located in the neck, this gland produces hormones that control the metabolism.

5: **Thymus**
This produces hormones that help to keep T lymphocytes healthy. The thymus is largest in children and shrinks during puberty.

6: **Adrenal glands (or suprarenal glands)**
Above the kidneys, the adrenal glands produce the fight-or-flight hormone adrenaline. They also make hormones involved in regulating blood pressure (aldosterone) and stress (cortisol).

7: **Ovaries (female only)**
The ovaries secrete female sex hormones, such as estrogen, that are involved in controlling the female menstrual cycle and in pregnancy.

8: **Testes (male only)**
The testes secrete male hormones such as testosterone, an important substance for sperm production, increasing bone and muscle size, and the growth of body hair.

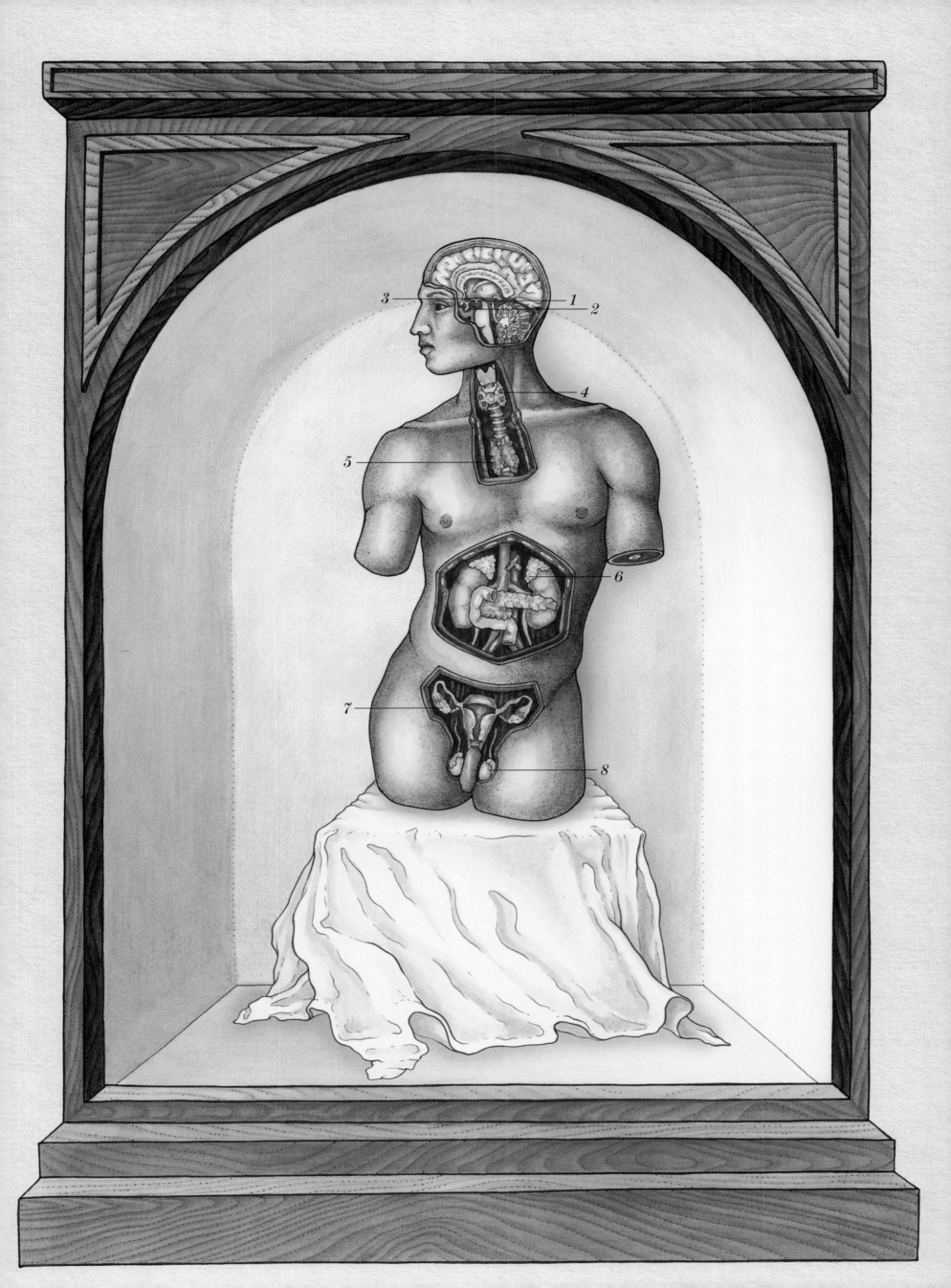

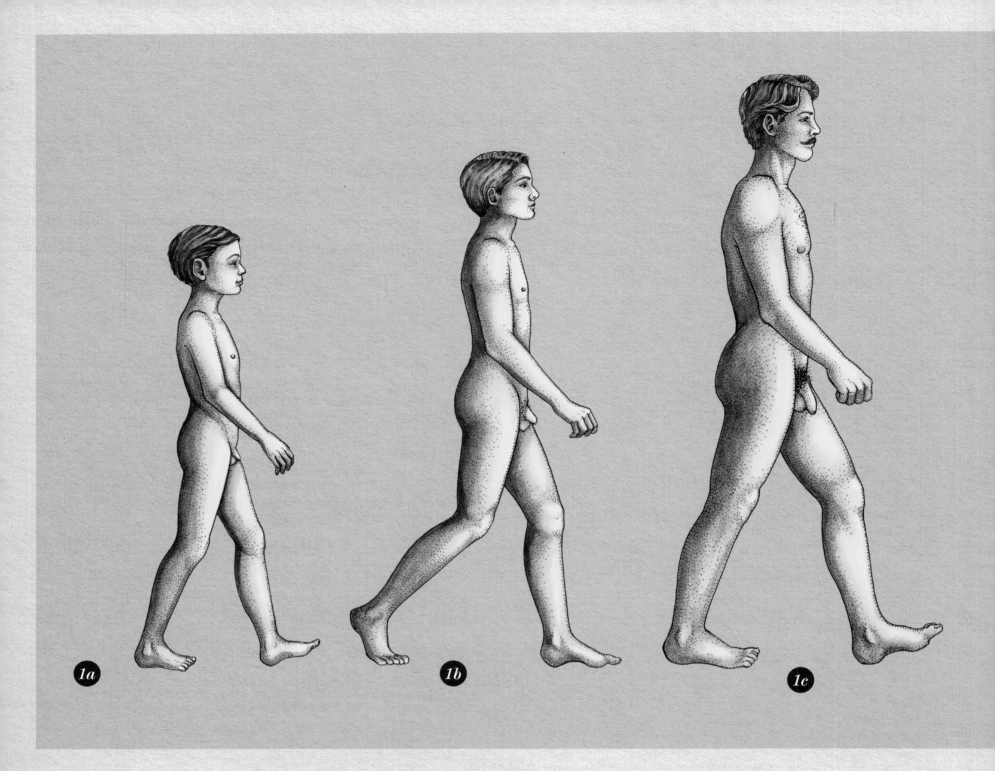

Puberty

As we transition from childhood to adulthood, the human body goes through an enormous change in growth, appearance, and feelings. This transition is called puberty and is triggered by hormones increasing their production and coursing through the body. Puberty most often begins between the ages of eight and fourteen, but it's different for everyone!

Puberty begins when the hypothalamus in the brain triggers the production of hormones by the pituitary gland. One of these is growth hormone, a chemical that makes bones grow in size. This means that during puberty children can have many growth spurts, growing as much as 4 inches/10 centimeters a year! Around the same time, more hormones begin to be produced in other endocrine glands (see page 82), stimulating hair growth. This leads to additional hair appearing all over the body, but in particular around the pubic region and the armpits.

Sex hormones—estrogen and testosterone—are produced by the reproductive organs, causing them to develop into their mature forms, capable of reproduction. In male-bodied people the reproductive organs start to make sperm, and in female-bodied people the menstrual cycle begins, and the ovary releases an egg every month that can be fertilized to develop into a baby.

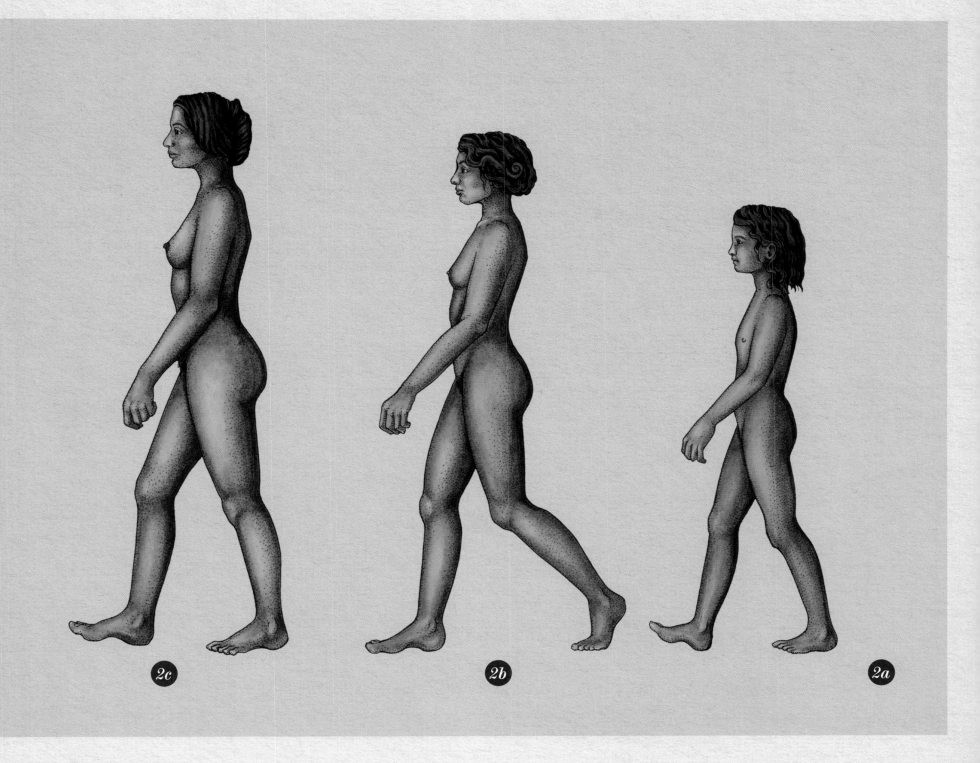

2c   2b   2a

The increase in hormones also affects overall body shape. Boys tend to develop broad shoulders and muscular frames, while girls may acquire more rounded bodies as their breasts and hips change shape. Boys might also find that their voice deepens or "cracks." Acne may develop as the surge of hormones increases the oiliness of the skin and causes a rise in sweat production. Alongside physical changes, huge fluctuations in hormones also have an effect on emotional responses. Sudden, intense changes in feelings, or mood swings, are common, and people will often begin to experience sexual attraction to others.

Key to plate

1: **Effects of puberty on the male body**
a) Prepubescent male
b) Pubescent body: At around ten to fifteen years old, people grow taller, their sex organs develop, body hair increases, and the voice deepens.
c) Adult body: After puberty, male bodies are typically taller and more muscular, with fully developed sex organs.

2: **Effects of puberty on the female body**
a) Prepubescent female
b) Pubescent body: At around ten to fifteen years old, people grow taller and start to develop breasts, organs develop, and the menstrual cycle may begin. Hair growth also increases and the body shape becomes more rounded.
c) Adult body: After puberty, breasts are fully developed and sex organs are capable of carrying a baby.

The Male Reproductive System

Every year around 125 million babies are born. Reproduction is nature's way of ensuring a population continues, and an individual's way of ensuring their genes are passed on. It occurs when male sex cells (sperm) and female sex cells (eggs) fuse together as a result of sexual intercourse. These two cells are the start of a whole new life.

The main job of the male reproductive system is to make sperm. Once a male-bodied person reaches puberty, sex hormones surge through the blood, reaching the testes and triggering sperm production. Hundreds of millions of sperm are made each day. During intercourse, they are released from the testes and travel down the thin tube of the urethra to the end of the penis. Along the way, the sperm mix with other fluids to make a liquid called semen, which then leaves the body quickly during ejaculation.

Sperm can only be made at temperatures a few degrees lower than the normal body temperature of 98.6°F/37°C, so the testes hang outside of the body in a sac of skin called the scrotum. If the testes get too cool, muscles contract to pull the testes closer to the body and warm them up again. Too tiny to be seen without a microscope, sperm are some of the smallest cells in the human body. Each one looks like a little tadpole: it has a "head" containing all of its genetic information (the instructions that tell cells what to do and what to become) and a tail used to propel it forward. To fertilize an egg, a sperm has to swim 8 to 12 inches/20 to 30 centimeters through the female reproductive system—a journey equivalent to a human swimming 6 miles/ 10 kilometers, or about two hundred lengths of a swimming pool. Mitochondria, special cells near the head of the sperm, act like a battery, providing energy as it makes its long journey, while nutrient-rich semen also nourishes it. Up to 300 million sperm can be released at once, but after the first one reaches and penetrates the egg, a chemical reaction in the egg stops any other sperm from getting in.

Key to plate

1: **Testes**
The two testes are where sperm (male sex cells) are produced within thousands of tiny tubes called seminiferous tubules. The testes sit within a sac of skin called the scrotum.

2: **Epididymis and ductus deferens**
These tubes connect the testes to the urethra (where urine is also carried out of the body). They transport sperm toward the end of the penis.

3: **Seminal vesicles**
The two seminal vesicles produce fluid that nourishes the sperm and—together with fluid from the prostate gland—makes semen.

4: **Urethra**
This long tube travels through the penis and is the route for sperm (and urine) to exit the body.

5: **Penis**
Most of the time, the penis is soft, as it is made of a spongy type of tissue. The spongy tissue of the penis can fill with blood, making it stiff and easier to insert into a vagina and to release sperm.

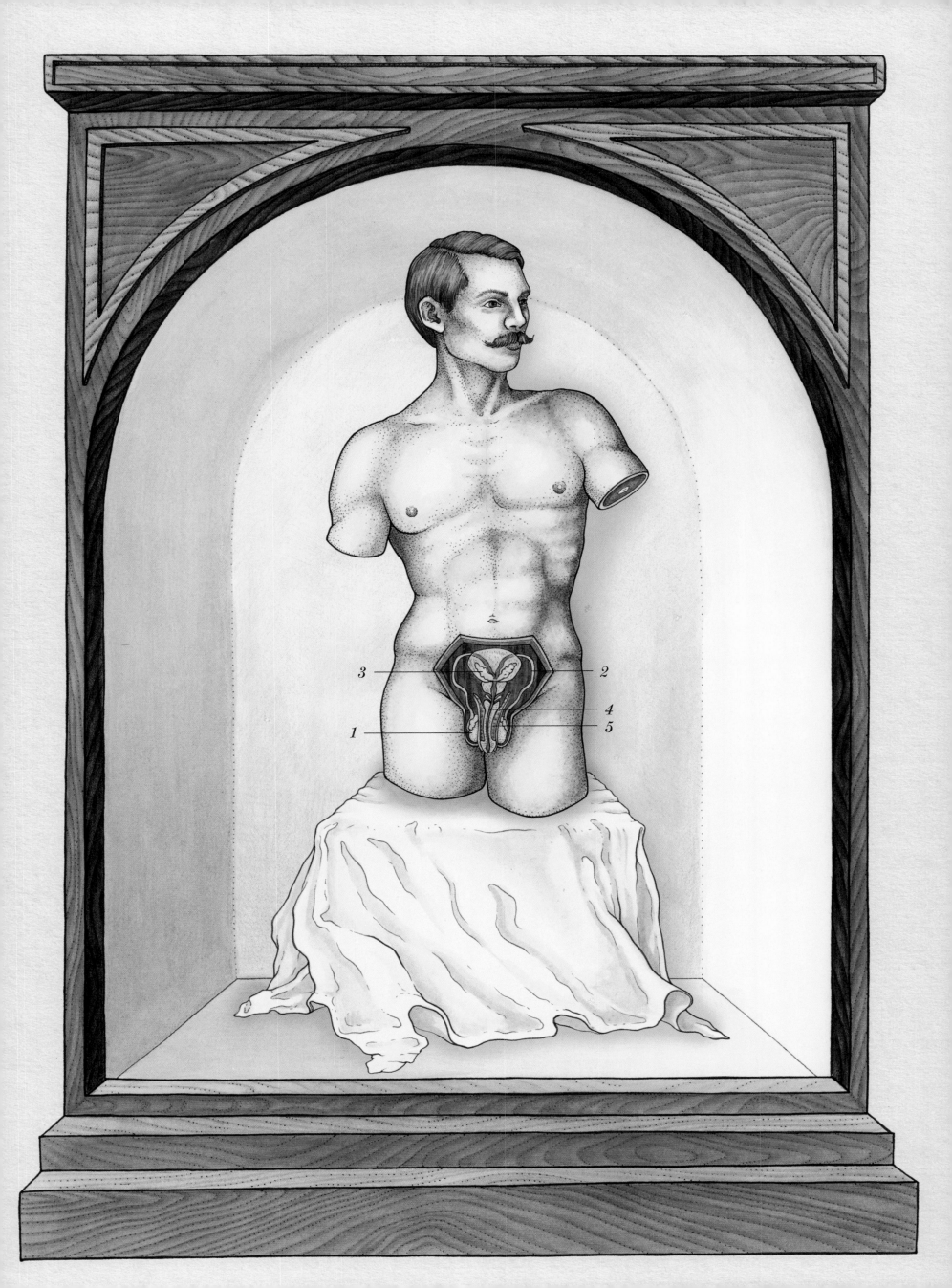

The Female Reproductive System

The role of the female reproductive system is to produce female sex cells, called eggs, and—if an egg is fertilized by a sperm—to nourish, grow, and protect a baby during pregnancy. All the eggs are present at birth and no more are produced. Although the ovaries contain millions of immature eggs, only a few hundred of these will be capable of fertilization.

Sitting within the pelvis are two ovaries, small rounded organs about 1 to 2 inches/ 3 to 5 centimeters long. They produce eggs as well as the female sex hormones, estrogen and progesterone. Starting at puberty, an egg will be released once a month as part of the menstrual cycle. First, the egg will be caught in the finger-like projections called fimbriae at the end of the uterine tube, a long muscular passageway that connects the ovary to the uterus. Once in the uterine tube, the egg can be fertilized by a sperm. Continuing its journey, the egg moves through the tube toward the uterus, a muscular organ in the pelvis. If the egg has been fertilized, it may embed itself within the lining of the uterus and begin to grow. When this happens, special hormones signal to the body to release other hormones to support the growth of the egg into a baby. If the egg is not fertilized, the uterine lining is shed. This is called menstruation.

The uterus is normally around 3 inches/7 centimeters long, about the size of a pear, but during pregnancy it grows to the size of a watermelon, large enough to hold a baby. It is made from smooth muscle, and during birth the walls of the uterus contract strongly to help push the baby out of the vagina. The vagina is also the route where sperm enters the body.

Key to plate

1: Ovary
Two ovaries sit in the female pelvis and produce eggs (female sex cells).

2: Uterine tube
Two uterine tubes connect to the uterus, transporting the egg that is released from the ovary. Fertilization of the egg by sperm often occurs in the uterine tube.

3: Uterus
This small muscular organ within the pelvis is where a fertilized egg will embed and develop into a baby.

4: Cervix
The boundary between the vagina and the uterus

5: Vagina
The vagina is a muscular canal connecting the uterus to the outer part of the genitals. Although not seen here, the external genitals (vulva) include the labia (lips) and the clitoris. The vagina is utilized during intercourse, menstruation, and childbirth.

6: Breast
Two breasts are found on the chest. They are mainly composed of fatty tissues, but also contain specialized tissue that produces milk. This is where breast milk used to feed newborn babies is produced.

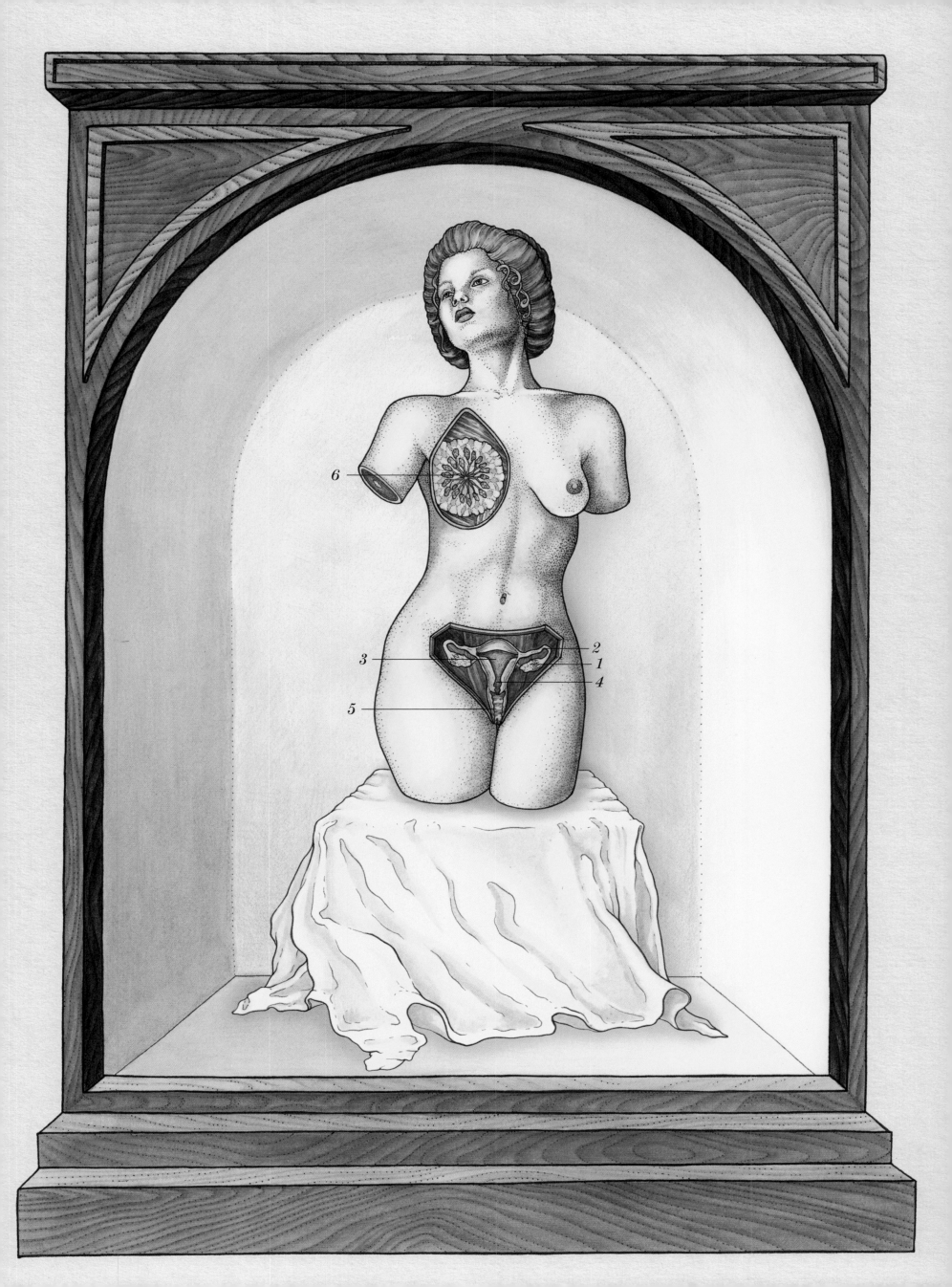

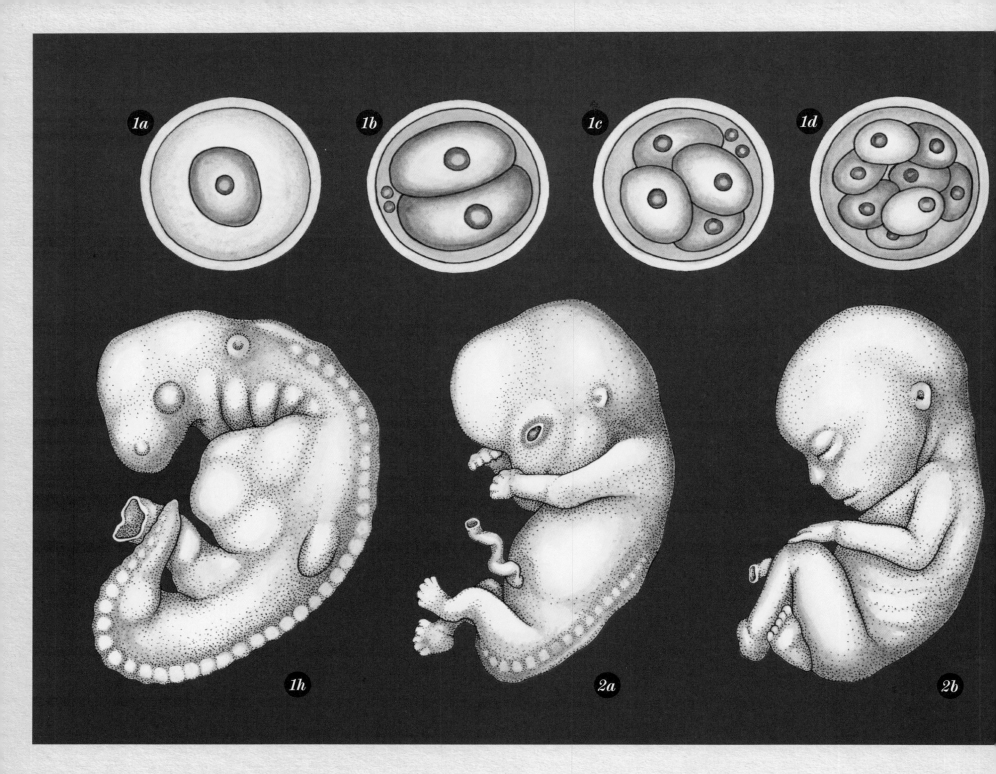

Development of a Baby

Fertilization usually occurs when a sperm meets an egg in one of the uterine tubes, a day or so after the egg is released from the ovary. The sperm burrows into the egg, combining their genetic information and making a new, unique individual.

Once the egg has been fertilized, it is called a zygote and begins to divide into two cells. These cells keep dividing and dividing until a ball of cells is made. The ball implants itself into the lining of the uterus, where it will be safe and secure. During pregnancy, the baby is surrounded by a sac of amniotic fluid, which keeps it protected. Nutrients and oxygen are passed from mother to baby by the placenta. This round organ forms in the uterus during pregnancy and connects to the baby via the long umbilical cord. It produces hormones (see page 82) that help the baby grow. After birth the cord is cut, and its remnants make the child's umbilicus or "belly button."

By six weeks, the developing baby is the size of an apple seed and has the beginnings

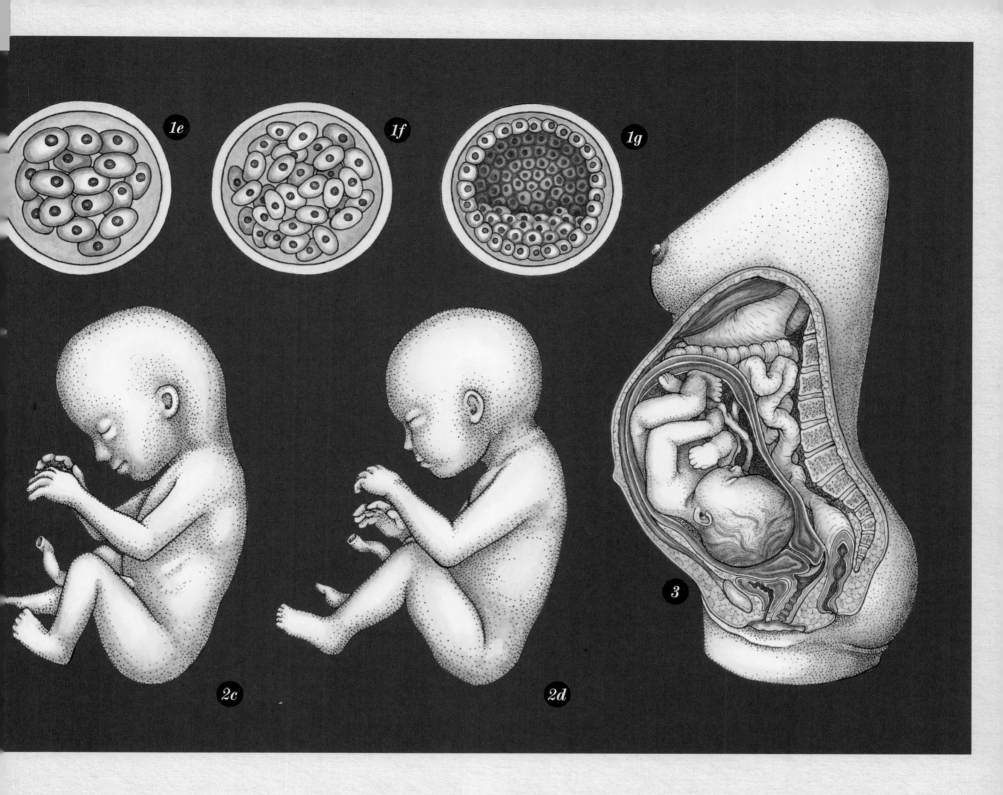

of limbs, a brain, and eyes. At eight weeks, the bean-sized baby is growing quickly and all of its major organs have started to form. By twenty weeks, the baby can begin to hear external sounds and the mother can feel its movements inside the uterus. The average length of pregnancy is forty weeks, but anywhere between thirty-seven and forty-two weeks is normal. When a baby is ready to be born, the muscles of the uterus squeeze (contract) in preparation for pushing the baby out through the vagina. These contractions get progressively more powerful, regular, and painful until the baby is born.

───────── *Key to plate* ─────────

1: **Embryonic development**
a) Fertilized egg (zygote): The fertilized egg begins to divide into more cells to form an embryo.
b) Two-cell stage
c) Four-cell stage
d) Eight-cell stage
e) Sixteen-cell stage (morula)
f) Thirty-two-cell stage
g) Blastocyst: By day five or six, the egg contains hundreds of cells, and is ready to implant inside the uterus.

h) End of week four: The embryo has started to form, and the beginnings of the head and limbs can be identified.

2: **Fetal development**
Now called a fetus, the developing baby has all of its major organs and will begin to grow in size.
a) Week nine (1 inch/2.5 centimeters long)
b) Week twelve (2 inches/ 5 centimeters long)

c) Week fifteen (4 inches/ 10 centimeters long)
d) Week twenty-five (13 inches/ 34 centimeters long)

3: **Full-term baby**
Between thirty-nine and forty weeks, the now fully developed baby is ready to be born. Strong contractions of the uterus will push the baby out of the vaginal canal.

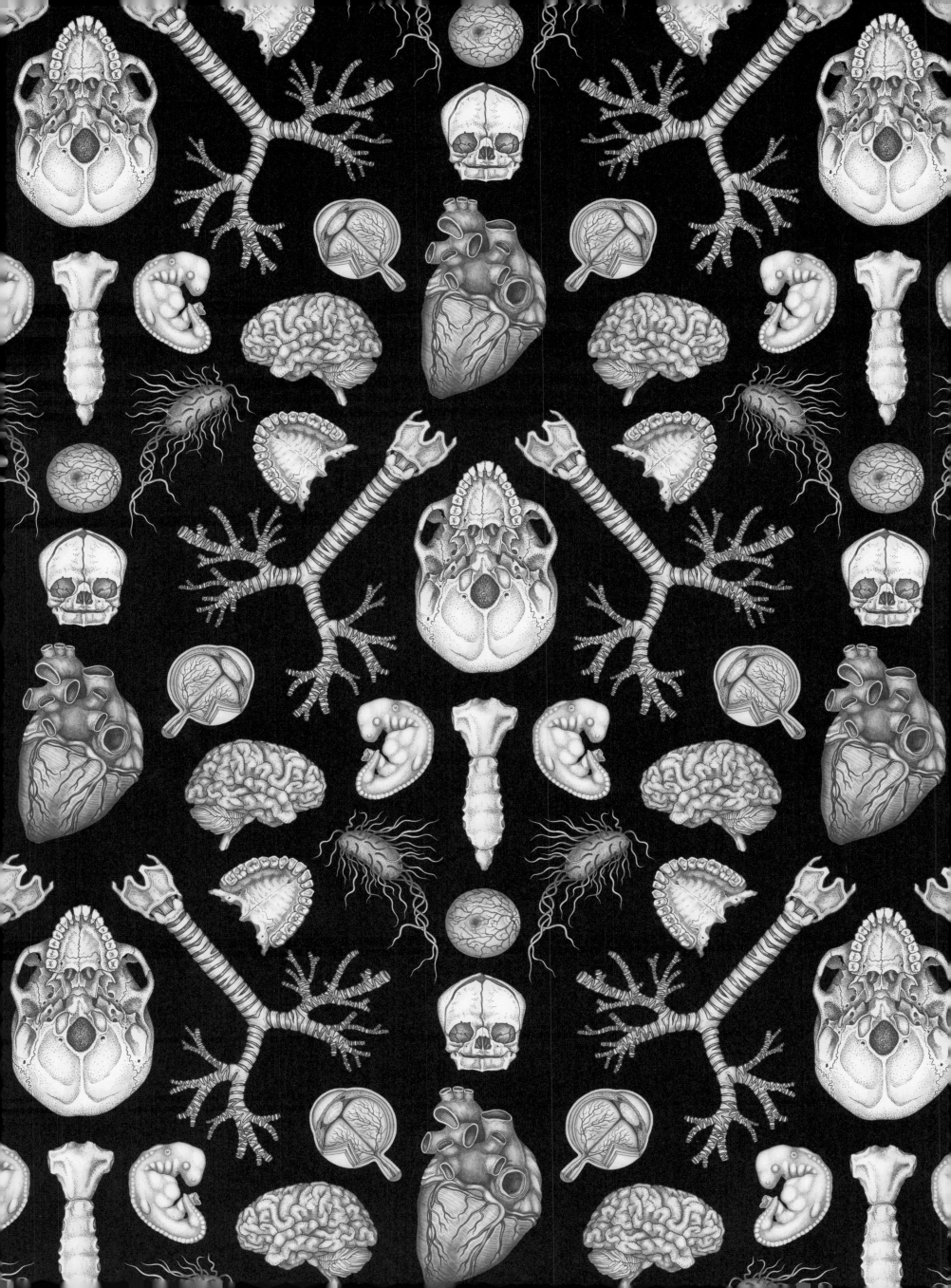

Library

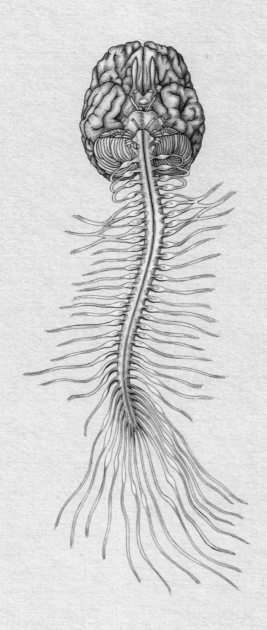

Index

Curators

To Learn More

Index

Curators

Katy Wiedemann is an illustrator and tattoo artist in Philadelphia. Her work explores the field of scientific illustration, particularly that of human and animal anatomy. Inspired by the great anatomical illustrators of history, she seeks to revisit the aesthetic of classic scientific illustration, but with a modern interpretation. Working in ink and watercolor, she uses traditional techniques to realize her blend of realism and scientific understanding and to highlight the beauty and complexity of our biological forms. She earned a BFA in illustration from the Rhode Island School of Design, as well as an MA in illustration from Edinburgh College of Art.

Jennifer Z. Paxton is lecturer in anatomy at the University of Edinburgh. She teaches anatomy to medical and science students and is also the principal investigator of the Paxton Lab, a tissue engineering laboratory focused on building new tissues of the musculoskeletal system for implantation after injury or disease. Jennifer is a keen science communicator and has won the Wellcome Trust "I'm a Scientist" competition twice (2013, 2018). She loves bringing the science of anatomy and tissue engineering to a wider audience and is currently working with primary schools to engage more children with these subjects.

To Learn More

BBC Bitesize Human Body
Excellent resources and quizzes for school-aged children.
www.bbc.com/bitesize/topics/zcyycdm

BBC Science & Nature: Human Body and Mind
Readers can find out all about their brain, heart, lungs, and various systems and get to know themselves better by taking psychological tests.
www.bbc.co.uk/science/humanbody/

British Heart Foundation: How Your Heart Works
Videos and information about the heart and circulatory system provided by the British Heart Foundation. You can also read about their latest research.
www.bhf.org.uk/informationsupport/how-a-healthy-heart-works

Encyclopaedia Britannica
Britannica's human body pages provide an accessible and encyclopedic covering of the facts.
www.britannica.com/science/human-body

Get Body Smart
Get Body Smart offers free tutorials and quizzes about human anatomy and physiology.
www.getbodysmart.com

Innerbody
Innerbody's Anatomy Explorer tool features over one thousand interactive anatomy maps for students to explore.
www.innerbody.com/htm/body.html

Teach Me Anatomy
Higher-level anatomy information is organized into anatomical regions.
www.teachmeanatomy.info

Wellcome Collection
Explore the Wellcome Collection's online image gallery, including anatomy illustrations through the ages.
www.wellcomecollection.org/works

ZygoteBody
Students can switch off the layers on this 3-D body to view individual organs.
www.zygotebody.com

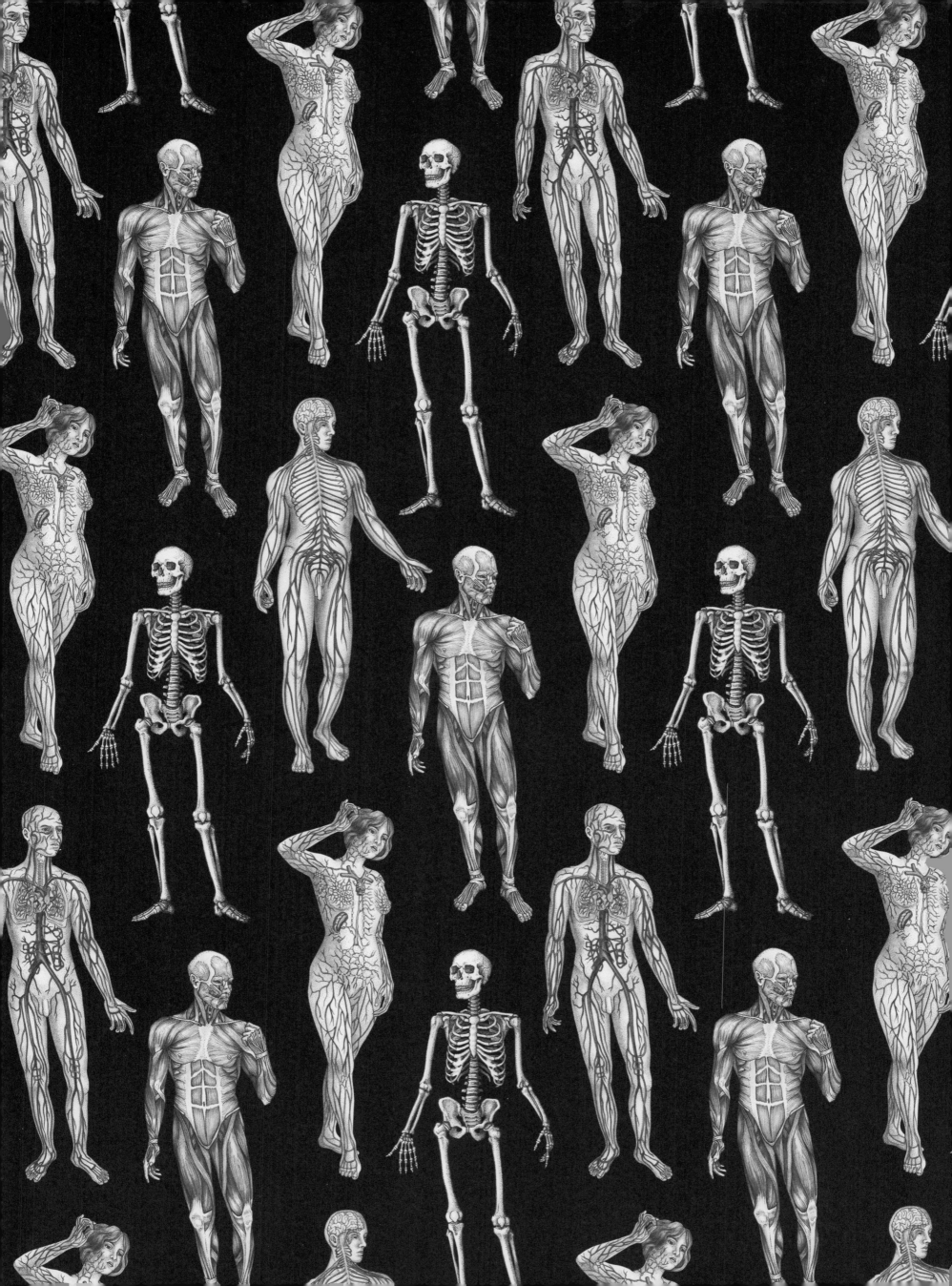

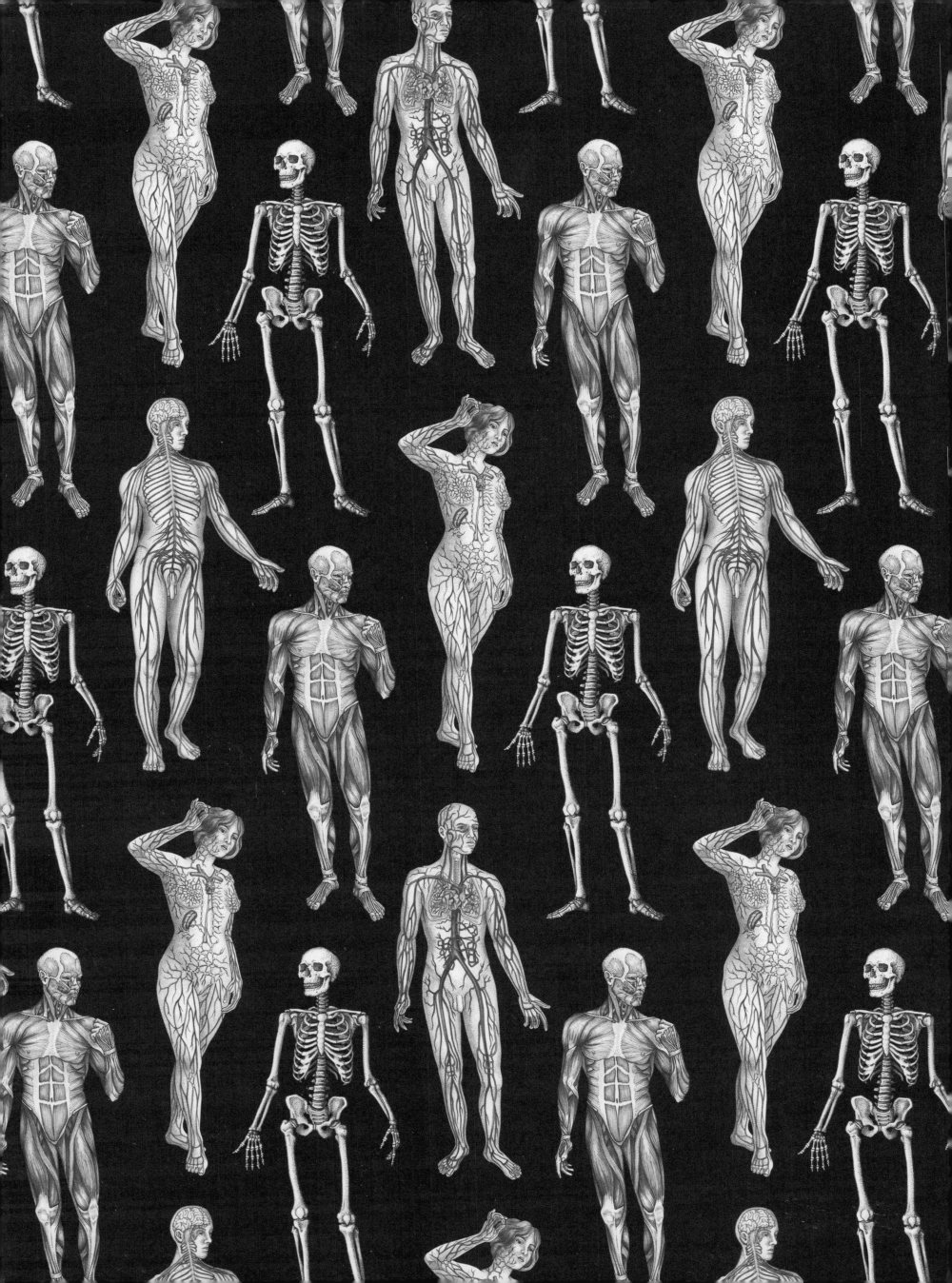

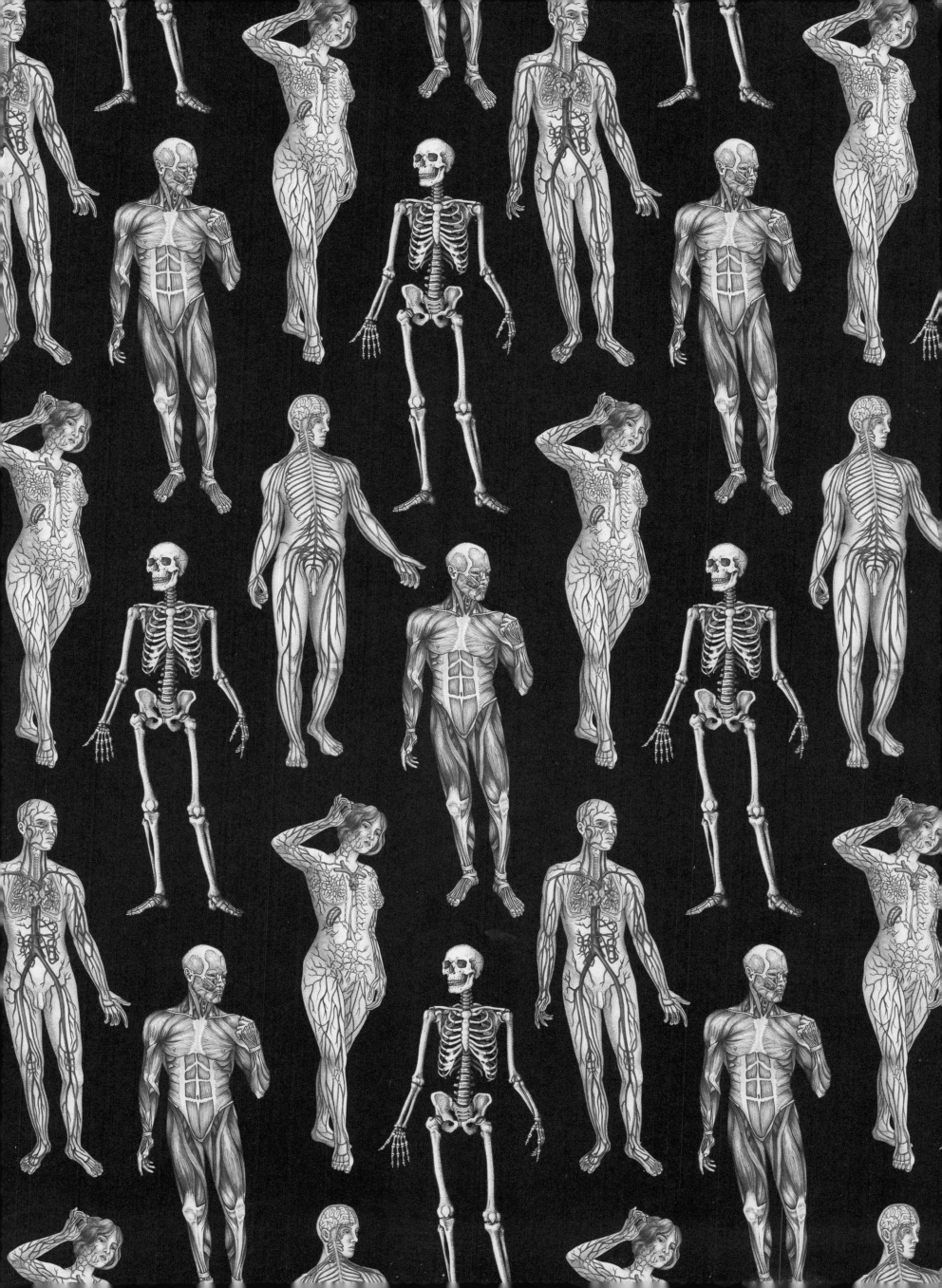

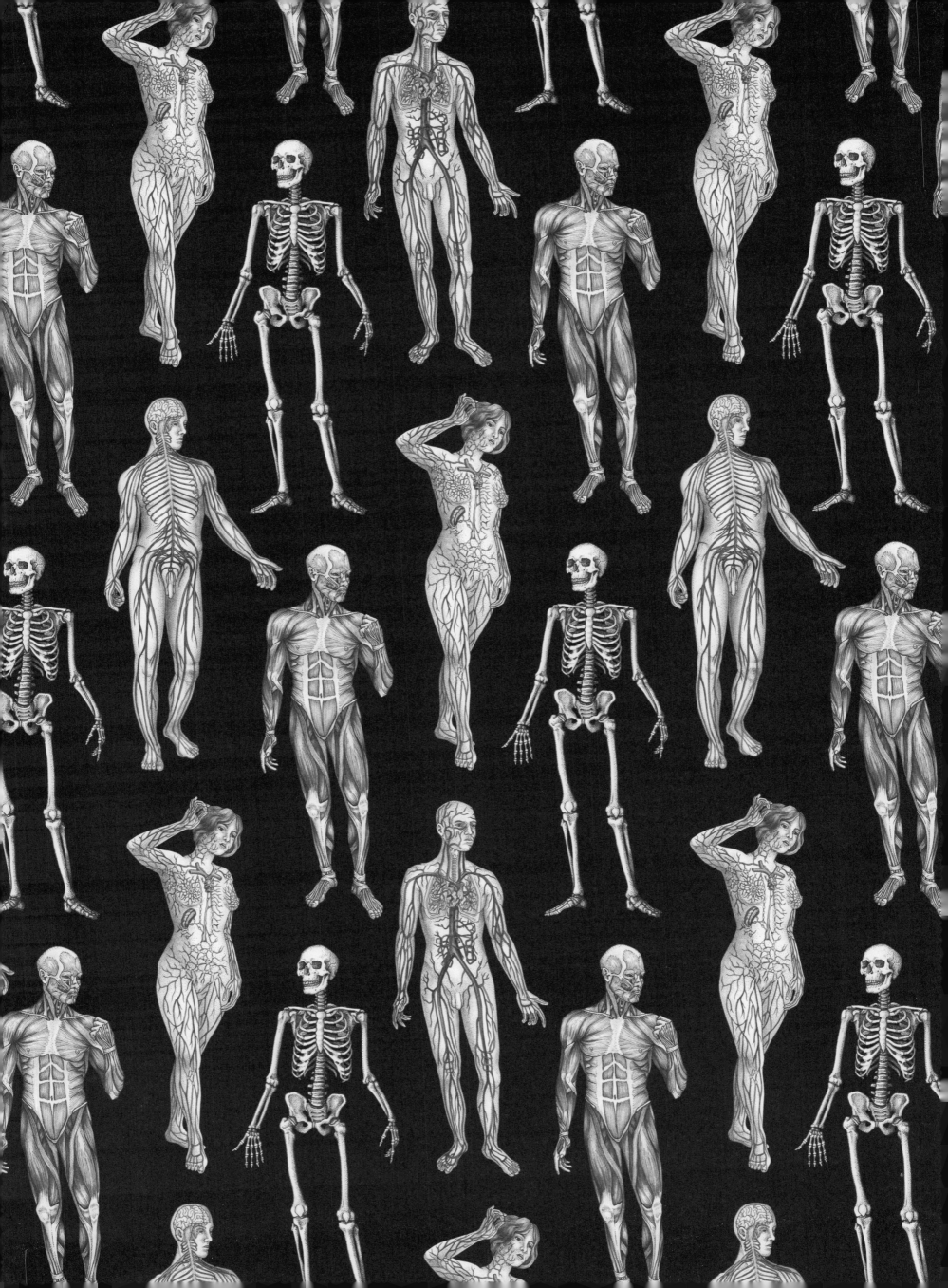